PSHE EDUCATION FOR KS3

Lesley de Meza
Stephen De Silva

Acknowledgements: photos

p.6 *tl* © Monkey Business – Fotolia, *bl* © Jacek Chabraszewski – Fotolia, *c* © bst2012 – Fotolia, *tr* © ErdalTorun – Fotolia, *br* © Comstock Images/Stockbyte/Thinkstock; **p.10** *l* © VIEW Pictures Ltd/Alamy, *r* © bizoo_n – Fotolia; **p.11** © Ruth D'Rozario; **p.13** *tl* © Design Pics Inc./Alamy, *c* © Getty Images/iStockphoto/Thinkstock, *br* © Monkey Business – Fotolia.com; **p.23** *A* © areeya_ann – Fotolia, *B* © Imagedoc/Alamy, *C* © Voisin/Phanie/Rex, *D* © HamsterMan – Fotolia, *E* © Saturn Stills/Science Photo Library, *F* © Africa Studio – Fotolia, *b* © Image Source Plus/Alamy; **p.25** *l* ©200606473 – Fotolia, *c* © Theo Wargo/WireImage/Getty Images, *r* © Ted Aljibe/AFP/Getty Images; **p.32** © Janine Wiedel Photolibrary/Alamy; **p.34** © Kevin Peterson/Photodisc/Getty Images; **p.38** © arrakasta – Fotolia; **p.40** *l* © Carlush – Fotolia, *c* © Khorzhevska – Fotolia, *r* © Lisa F. Young – Fotolia; **p.41** *t* © Fotomicar – Fotolia, *ct* © Steph Fowler/Stockbyte/Getty Images, *cb* © PhotosIndia.com LLC/Alamy, *b* © Eric Limon – Fotolia; **p.43** © Getty Images/iStockphoto/Thinkstock; **p.54** *t* © Darrin Jenkins/Alamy, *c* © Imagestate Media (John Foxx), *bl* © swa182 – Fotolia, *br* © Rex Features; **p.55** *tl* © SAKKI/Rex Features, *tc* © Photographee.eu – Fotolia; *tr* © Joe Bird/Alamy, *cr* © Getty Images/iStockphoto/Thinkstock, *br* © Getty Images/iStockphoto/Thinkstock; **p.65** © Sabphoto – Fotolia; **p.68** *tl* © Peter Barritt/Alamy, *tr* © Ulrich Doering/Alamy, *bl* © Dan Race – Fotolia, *br* © Digitalpress – Fotolia; **p.71** © Julian Finney/Getty Images; **p.72** © Larry Marano/Getty Images; **p.73** © Monkey Business – Fotolia; **p.77** © David Bebber/WPA Pool/Getty Images; **p.87** *tl* © Alexander Raths – Fotolia, *tr* © Tyler Olson – Fotolia, *bl* © Voisin/Phanie/Rex Features, *br* © Creativa – Fotolia; **p.88** *l* © Péter Mács – Fotolia, *c* © wawritto – Fotolia, *tr* © Getty Images/Fuse/Thinkstock, *br* © Romanchuck – Fotolia; **p.91** *tl* © william87 – Fotolia, *cr* © plotnik – Fotolia, *bl* © Taigi – Fotolia; **p.96** *l* © alephnull – Fotolia, *c* © CandyBox Images – Fotolia, *r* © Eric Gevaert – Fotolia; **p.97** © Val Thoermer – Fotolia; **p.99** *t* © Paul Hebditch/Alamy, *c* © Michael Brown – Fotolia, *b* © piai – Fotolia; **p.102** © dja65 – Fotolia; **p.103** © John Carey/Getty Images; **p.104** Reproduced with kind permission of Women's Aid; **p.108** *t* Reproduced with kind permission of the Office of the Children's Commissioner, *b* Reproduced with the kind permission of the NSPCC; **p.112** *l* © Getty Images/Creatas RF/Thinkstock, *cl* © Getty Images/Image Source, *tr* © Hogan Imaging – Fotolia, *br* © Rob – Fotolia; **p.114** *t* © JPC-PROD – Fotolia, *ct* © oporkka – Fotolia.com, *cb* © igor – Fotolia, *b* © igor – Fotolia; **p.117** *t* © Syda Productions – Fotolia, *b* © Katrina Miller – Fotolia; **p.122** *l* © poco_bw – Fotolia, *r* © Wang Hsiu-Hua – Fotolia; **p.123** *tl* © Wong Sze Fei – Fotolia, *tr* © Michael Flippo – Fotolia, *bl* © Howard Sandler – Fotolia, *br* © Yuri Arcurs – Fotolia; **p.124** *l* © creative soul – Fotolia, *c* © boston_g – Fotolia, *r* © grafikplusfoto – Fotolia; **p.125** © Rex Features; **p.127** *t* © Jon Stroud/Rex Features, *b* © Rex Features; **p.128** © Monkey Business – Fotolia; **p.129** © diversepixel – Fotolia; **pp.130–1** © Tetra images/Getty Images; **p.132** © Bubbles Photolibrary/Alamy; **p.137** Reproduced with the kind permission of Aghalee Village Hall; **p.139** *t* Reproduced with the kind permission of the Anti-Bullying Alliance, *ct* Reproduced with the kind permission of the NSPCC, *c* Reproduced with the kind permission of a kidspace, *cb* Reproduced with the kind permission of Thinkuknow/National Crime Agency, CEOP Command, *b* Reproduced with the kind permission of YoungMinds; **p.140** *t* © Bikeworldtravel – Fotolia, *b* © kmiragaya – Fotolia; **p.142** © Timothy Tadder/Punchstock/Corbis; **p.145** *tl* © auremar – Fotolia, *tr* © britta60 – Fotolia, *bl* © Kadmy – Fotolia, *br* © Image Source/Alamy; **p.146** © michaeljung – Fotolia.com; **p.153** © Andy Dean – Fotolia; **p.156** *tl* © Deklofenak – Fotolia, *tc* © pio3 – Fotolia, *tr* © emde71 – Fotolia.com, *bl* © Getty Images/Hemera/Thinkstock, *bc* © Digital Vision/Photodisc/Thinkstock; **p.157** *t* © singkham – Fotolia, *b* © JPC-PROD – Fotolia; **p.162** *tl* © Anna Stowe/Alamy, *tc* © Greg Balfour Evans/Alamy, *tr* © Travel Pictures/Alamy, *bl* © Minerva Studio – Fotolia, *br* © Alex Segre/Alamy; **p.163** *l* © Anna Stowe/Alamy, *cl* © Greg Balfour Evans/Alamy, *c* © Travel Pictures/Alamy, *cr* © Minerva Studio – Fotolia, *r* © Alex Segre/Alamy; **p.164** *l* © The Wand Company, *r* © Nick Cunard/Rex Features; **p.166** © Rex Features.

l = left, *r* = right, *c* = centre, *t* = top, *b* = bottom

Please note all photos are posed by models except pp.25, 71, 72, 77, 125, 127, 164 and 166.

Acknowledgements: text

p.39 Pornography survey; screenshot, images and text from http://s.telegraph.co.uk/graphics/html/Years/2013/September/images/sexEducation.png, © Telegraph Media Group Limited 2013, reproduced by permission of Telegraph Media Group; **p.45** 'Personal safety: your rights', adapted from http://www.brook.org.uk/index.php/sex-relationships/harmful-situations/abuse; **p.49** 'Young people and drugs - fact or fiction?', public health statistics from NHS Health and Social Care Information Centre, 2005-2012; **p.71** 'David Weir, Paralympic superman', from NHS Choices, http://www.nhs.uk/Livewell/fitness/Pages/david-weir-paralympics.aspx, © Crown Copyright 2013, Department of Health; **p.72** Jeffrey M. Elliot, *Conversations with Maya Angelou* (Virago, 1989), copyright © 1989 by the University Press of Mississippi; **p.86** Summary guide by the Children's Rights Alliance of England, from http://www.crae.org.uk/rights/uncrc.html; **p.103** 'Child sexual exploitation: Myth vs. reality', © Local Government Association, June 2013; Tom Parry, 'You can be ex-gang but you can never be an ex murderer: Tough USA-style scheme helps youth quit', from http://www.mirror.co.uk/news/real-life-stories/you-can-ex-gang-you-2081507 (*Daily Mirror*, July 23, 2013), reproduced by permission of Mirrorpix; **p.105** EMF – The Social Justice Foundation, 'Lena's Story' (Case Study 1) and 'Raj's Story' (Case Study 4), from http://www.forcedmarriage.net.

Permission for re-use of all © Crown copyright information is granted under the terms of the Open Government Licence (OGL).

Although every effort has been made to ensure that website addresses are correct at time of going to press, Hodder Education cannot be held responsible for the content of any website mentioned in this book. It is sometimes possible to find a relocated web page by typing in the address of the home page for a website in the URL window of your browser.

Hachette UK's policy is to use papers that are natural, renewable and recyclable products and made from wood grown in sustainable forests. The logging and manufacturing processes are expected to conform to the environmental regulations of the country of origin.

Orders: please contact Bookpoint Ltd, 130 Milton Park, Abingdon, Oxon OX14 4SB. Telephone: +44 (0)1235 827720. Fax: +44 (0)1235 400454. Lines are open 9.00a.m.–5.00p.m., Monday to Saturday, with a 24-hour message answering service. Visit our website at www.hoddereducation.co.uk

© Lesley de Meza, Stephen De Silva 2014

First published in 2014 by

Hodder Education,

An Hachette UK Company

338 Euston Road

London NW1 3BH

Impression number 10 9 8 7 6 5 4 3 2 1

Year   2018 2017 2016 2015 2014

Cover photo © Roman Borodaev/Alamy

Illustrations by Barking Dog, Peter Lubach, Oxford Illustrators

Typeset in Frutiger LT Std 45 Light 11/14pt by Integra Software Services Pvt. Ltd., Pondicherry, India

Printed in Italy

A catalogue record for this title is available from the British Library

ISBN 9781471808470

Introduction for teachers: Personal, Social, Health and Economic (PSHE) Education

PSHE Education for Key Stage 3 is a planned programme of learning opportunities and experiences that help young people grow and develop as individuals, and as members of families and of social and economic communities.

This course should be used in the context of a whole-school approach to meet the statutory aims of the curriculum to which PSHE education is essential. The aims are to enable all young people to become:

- successful learners who enjoy learning, make progress and achieve
- confident individuals who are able to live safe, healthy and fulfilling lives
- responsible citizens who make a positive contribution to society.

Section 2.1 of the National Curriculum framework states that all schools have statutory duties:
Every state-funded school must offer a curriculum which is balanced and broadly based and which:

- *promotes the spiritual, moral, cultural, mental and physical development of pupils at the school and of society*
- *prepares pupils at the school for the opportunities, responsibilities and experiences of later life…*

Schools also have statutory responsibilities regarding pupil wellbeing and safeguarding (Children Act 2004) and community cohesion (Education Act 2006). PSHE education plays an important part in fulfilling all of these responsibilities.

About the course

This course includes the following resources:

- This pupil book which covers topics from the PSHE Association's revised Programme of Study across 11 chapters
- Activity worksheets, available for free on http://bit.do/PSHE, to support various activities in this book.
- Teacher's notes and more worksheets, images, interactive activities and weblinks, for all chapters, as part of *PSHE Education Dynamic Learning Teaching and Learning Resources*. Please visit www.hoddereducation.co.uk/Dynamic-Learning to find out more and sign up for a free 30-day trial.

About this book

Each chapter is made up of a series of lessons. The chapters are numbered for ease of use but can be used in any order, for example, 'Relationships and sex education' can be found in Chapters 2 and 3. However, you may decide to cover this topic at different times in each year group.

The lessons in each chapter are organised into three year groups: 7, 8 and 9. Within any chapter's lessons for a single year group, you will find it best to do each lesson in order, as they have been designed to be progressive.

The lessons are colour-coded for ease of reference:
blue for Year 7
red for Year 8
green for Year 9.

This allows for the 'spiral curriculum' approach which revisits topics each year at a different developmental stage. Research into PSHE identifies the spiral curriculum as an essential component of effective teaching and learning.

Confidentiality

Some PSHE topics will need to be treated with sensitivity in class, but teachers cannot and should not promise total confidentiality. The boundaries of confidentiality should be made clear to pupils. If a pupil discloses information which is sensitive, not generally known, and which the pupil asks not to be passed on, the request should be honoured unless this is unavoidable in order for teachers to fulfil their professional responsibilities in relation to: Safeguarding/Child Protection; co-operating with a police investigation; or referral to external services.

Contents

Chapter 1 Introducing PSHE education

1.1 What is PSHE? 6
1.2 How will we work together? 8
1.3 How is Year 7 different? 10
1.4 What's it like here? 12
1.5 What do I value and why? 14

Chapter 2 Relationships and sex education: facts

2.1 What happens at puberty? 18
2.2 How are babies made? 20
2.3 What is contraception? 22
2.4 What are HIV and AIDS? 24
2.5 What are STIs? 26
2.6 What does the law say? 28

Chapter 3 Relationships and sex education: feelings

3.1 Why am I feeling like this? 30
3.2 Boys and girls – is there a difference? 32
3.3 Why are friends important? 34
3.4 What are the different types of relationships? 36
3.5 What do we see about sex in the media? 38
3.6 Is commitment important in relationships? 40
3.7 What if I don't want to? 42

Chapter 4 Drugs

4.1 What do we mean by 'drugs'? 46
4.2 Drugs – fact or fiction? 48
4.3 How do drugs affect people? 50
4.4 What about drugs and the law? 54
4.5 How do I manage situations involving drugs? 56

Chapter 5 Emotional wellbeing

5.1 What am I good at? 60
5.2 What does 'assertiveness' mean? 62
5.3 What happens when we are feeling down? 64
5.4 What does 'resilience' mean? 66
5.5 Is anybody perfect? 68
5.6 How do I manage my feelings? 70
5.7 What happens when relationships break down? 74
5.8 How do we cope with loss and bereavement? 76

Chapter 6 Healthy lifestyle

6.1 What do we need to keep healthy? 78
6.2 What is my personal health profile? 80
6.3 How do I keep healthy? 82
6.4 Who can I talk to about my health? 86

Chapter 7 Risk and safety

7.1 What do we mean by 'risk'?	88
7.2 How do we manage risky situations?	90
7.3 How do I practise refusal skills?	92
7.4 How can we tackle bullying?	94
7.5 What is 'risking on purpose'?	96
7.6 Can gambling be good?	98
7.7 How do I reduce risks?	100
7.8 Who can help me keep safe?	102
7.9 Where can I find help on …?	106

Chapter 8 Identity

8.1 Who am I?	110
8.2 What does 'family' mean?	112
8.3 How can I contribute to family life?	114
8.4 How do I respond to other people?	116
8.5 How am I doing?	118
8.6 What are my rights and responsibilities?	120

Chapter 9 Communities

9.1 Who is in our communities?	122
9.2 How do I feel about 'difference'?	124
9.3 How can we value each other?	126
9.4 What makes a successful community?	128
9.5 What can cause problems in communities?	132
9.6 How can I contribute to my community?	135
9.7 What do voluntary agencies do?	138
9.8 How can we challenge prejudice and discrimination?	140

Chapter 10 Planning for the future

10.1 How do I work best with others?	142
10.2 How can we improve our communication skills?	144
10.3 What do I want and how do I get it?	146
10.4 How do I plan for my future?	148
10.5 What do I need to plan for?	150
10.6 What opportunities are out there for me?	152
10.7 How do I improve my prospects?	154
10.8 What does the law say about work?	156

Chapter 11 Money and me

11.1 How do I save and how do I budget?	159
11.2 What influences our spending?	162
11.3 How enterprising am I?	164

Index

Index	168

1.1 What is PSHE?

Starter

Think back to when you were in Year 6. What did you enjoy, what were you looking forward to, and what did you worry about?

In small groups divide a large piece of paper into four sections with the headings:

1 We were worried about …
2 Outside school we enjoyed …
3 In school we enjoyed …
4 We were looking forward to …

Then fill in the sections with your ideas. Agree and feed back on the most important thing for each section.

The starter activity is what PSHE will be about: learning with each other and from each other. All of us learn and develop at school and in our wider lives outside school. We learn at school, in the playground, going shopping, at the movies – we may not realise it but we are learning all the time. This is part of what we call 'personal development'.

Activity 1

In pairs, look at the photos in Source 1. What personal development might be happening in each of the situations?

PERSONAL DEVELOPMENT = Life + The Universe + Everything

Source 1 Wherever we go, whoever we talk to, we are always learning

PSHE education lessons are just one place where we can think about things that are important to each of us, and how we live in the world.

The letters PSHE stand for:

Personal
Social
Health
Economic

Activity 2

The word bank below includes some of the topics you will be learning about in your PSHE course this year. In groups, organise the words under the PSHE headings (Personal, Social, Health and Economic). In your groups brainstorm some other topics you think might be covered under each of the headings.

Me and my family   Eating well   Saving pocket money   Feelings
Making choices   Donating to charity   Good communication
Not smoking   Exercise   Working with others   Friends

As well as learning about different topics, PSHE education is also about doing things.

Activity 3

Think back over the activities you have done in this lesson. Did they include using any of the skills on the checklist on the right?

✓ learning with each other

✓ learning from each other

✓ bringing your own ideas and thoughts

✓ sharing them together

✓ listening to each other

✓ finding out what you have in common

✓ thinking about what is important to you.

1.2 How will we work together?

In this lesson you will learn:
- about the values of PSHE education
- how to create a Group Agreement for everyone to work together in a safe and positive way.

We all have ideas by which we live, for example, 'it is important to help other people', 'we should treat other people the same way we would like to be treated', and so on. Sometimes we call these ideas 'values'.

Your PSHE education course can help you to develop a set of values – Source 1, the rainbow diagram, is an example of this.

Know that each of us is unique
Gain good information to make choices
Develop decision-making skills
Understand our emotions and feelings
Enjoy what we learn
Feel safe and supported to say what we think
Listen to and consider what other people say

Source 1 PSHE values

Starter

In pairs, look at the rainbow of PSHE values in Source 1 and identify one example that everyone could do to work within these values.

The values in Source 1 are one way of describing how you can work with each other in PSHE. Another is to use these to develop a Group Agreement. A Group Agreement outlines the rights and responsibilities you share.

In PSHE each of us has the right to …

Be heard.
_____

So each person also has the responsibility to …

Listen to others when they speak.
_____

In PSHE each of us has the right to …

_____

So each person also has the responsibility to …

_____

In PSHE each of us has the right to …

_____

So each person also has the responsibility to …

_____

Source 2 An example of a Group Agreement

Activity 1

Work together in small groups to come up with a Group Agreement. It should outline the rights and responsibilities you think you should share in PSHE. Use the example in Source 2 to help you.

All groups should feed back their ideas to everyone to help come up with a Group Agreement.

Activity 2

Can you think of examples of Group Agreements in everyday life? For example, the Highway Code is a Group Agreement which has become a law. A more informal example is the acceptance of speaking quietly and only when necessary in a library, allowing others to concentrate.

Children and young people in Scotland were asked to come up with a Charter setting out how they would like to be treated. The Charter in Source 3 is what they came up with.

Activity 3

If you were given the opportunity to ask adults in this country to listen to you, what would you include in your charter?

A Charter for Young People

Get to know us

Speak with us

Listen to us

Take us seriously

Involve us

Respect our privacy

Be responsible to us

Think about our lives as a whole

Think carefully about how you use information about us

Put us in touch with the right people

Use your power to help

Make things happen when they should

Help us be safe

Source 3 Protecting Children and Young People: The Charter (Scottish Executive)

1.3 How is Year 7 different?

In this lesson you will learn:
- about the changes you are experiencing as a secondary school pupil
- ways to support yourself and other pupils who are new to the school.

Starter

The photos in Source 1 show some ways in which a secondary school may look different from primary school. What rules are new to you here (compared to your last school)? Why do you think the rules are different?

Source 1 Secondary school

Activity 1

When we begin anything new in our lives it is normal to feel excited and/or worried, and lack confidence, all at the same time. You might have attended an induction/taster day before you came to your new school, when there was a lot to take in. You may not have wanted to ask questions. What most worried you about coming to a new school?

Activity 2

In Source 2 you can see some recommendations from pupils your age about how to make the change to a new school as smooth as possible. Choose the three that you think are the most important.

Activity 3

It's good to have a personal checklist to help you keep organised and happy at school. What kind of things would you put on your list?

Have confidence. Don't worry or be scared.

Be prepared/ organised – make sure you have the right equipment.

If someone is causing trouble or upsetting another person, don't join in.

Make new friends but don't forget your old ones.

Take advice from teachers and good friends.

Don't be afraid – reporting bullying (towards you or other people) is a good thing.

Get your homework in on time.

Listen to your teachers and do as you are told the first time.

Ask for help if you need it.

Be a good person – kind, nice, friendly and polite towards others.

Source 2 A guide to survive

Activity 4

Complete this sentence: 'My top tip to myself to be successful at my new school is …'

1.4 What's it like here?

In this lesson you will:
- review the changes you have experienced in the last year
- suggest ways of supporting pupils who are new to the school.

Starter

Think back to how you felt on your first day in Year 7. You probably feel different now but in many ways you are still the same person.

Complete these sentences, giving one reason for each:
1 We are the same as when we started in Year 7 because …
2 We are different from the way we were when we started in Year 7 because …

Many pupils arriving at secondary school do not know the buildings or people very well. Even if you had visited the school on some kind of orientation day, there was still a lot to take in.

Activity 1

Think back over the things you experienced in your first few weeks as a new Year 7 pupil. Does anything in particular stand out in your memory? Can you remember how it felt?

In the Starter Activity and Activity 1 you looked back at and started to think about what life was like in Year 7. Throughout the rest of this lesson you will think about the current Year 7 newcomers to the school and how you could help them.

Many people going on a holiday or to visit to a new place get a travel guide. The most useful guides are written by people who have actually experienced the place they are writing about. Imagine you had to write a guide to the school for a new Year 7 group. What things does a new Year 7 group need to know? What would be useful? Look at the examples on the next page.

Moving around between lessons

Names of the teachers

House/tutor and/or year group systems

Making new friends

Who to speak to if things go wrong

How the canteen works

Where and when assemblies are held

The layout of the school and classrooms

Activity 2

Your task is to write a guide to the school for a Year 7 pupil by following the steps below:

1 Make a list of things that you think are important to know about in this school. Use the examples on these two pages for ideas and come up with some of your own, which you may have discussed in Activity 1. Each item on this list will form a chapter of the guide.
2 Work together in small groups, each one planning one section of the guide. Make a list of the information that you think needs to be included.
3 Feed back your ideas to the rest of the class.

Activity 3

Consider all the different advice that the groups came up with in the previous activity. Discuss whether there are any useful recommendations that could be made to the School Council (or another group of pupils or staff responsible for Year 7) to help those who will join your school in the future.

Activity 4

In small groups, share with each other what you found most useful in helping you to settle in at this school.

1.5 What do I value and why?

In this lesson you will:
- think about what 'values' are
- consider what values you hold
- reflect on values you may share with other people.

When you hear the word 'value' you might think it simply means how much money something is worth. But the truth is we value all kinds of things in our lives, in lots of different ways. Think about whether or not any of these things are worth anything to you:
- Having a good friend
- Being able to talk to a family member you trust
- The pleasure you get from having a pet
- Finding time to watch TV or listen to music
- Having the freedom to express your opinion

Starter

Imagine someone who says:

I value planet Earth and have concerns about global warming – so I do my best to support organisations that stop the destruction of the rainforests. For example, I only use recycled paper.

This person has a value that affects the way they behave. What value or values do you hold that make you act in a certain way?

Most people have a range of values that influence the way they think, feel and behave. Some values will be more important to them than others.

Activity 1

Look at Source 1. It shows Zoe at the centre and around her are two circles showing six things she really values – three of them are particularly important and those are shown closest to her.
Construct your own values circle with you at the centre and two more rings of values surrounding you.

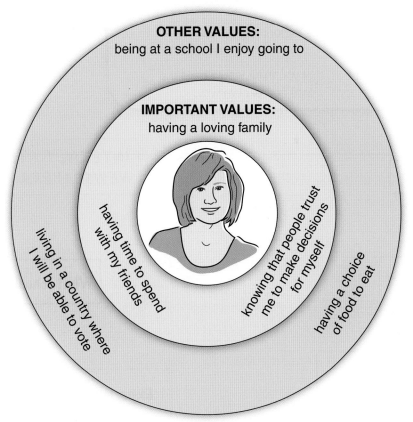

OTHER VALUES:
being at a school I enjoy going to

IMPORTANT VALUES:
having a loving family

living in a country where
I will be able to vote

having time to spend
with my friends

knowing that people trust
me to make decisions
for myself

having a choice
of food to eat

Source 1 A values circle

Activity 2

By now you will have a clearer idea of some of the things you value. This activity asks you to think about the bigger picture.

1 Look at the values listed below:
   a Being free to express our opinions
   b Enjoying ourselves
   c Having human rights
   d Feeling safe
   e Having rules and laws
   f Being free to have our own beliefs
   g Having good health services
   h Having respect
   i Being trusted

These are the values we often share in our communities and the society in which we live. Which of the values is most important to you?

2 Look at Source 2. It shows a Diamond Nine arrangement for placing your values in a priority order.

Sort the nine values listed above, placing the one of most value to you in position 1 and the one of least value in position 9.

3 Consider the nine values listed above and your own values that you identified in Activity 1. If you could only choose one to have in your life, what would your most prized value be – and why?

Source 2 Diamond Nine

Activity 3

Look at the list below. Which of these factors might influence a person's values?

Choose three factors from the list that you think would have the strongest influence on a person's values and explain why.

| Views of parents/carers | | INTERNET / TELEVISION / NEWSPAPERS |

Religious teachings

The law

Discussions with friends

What schools teach

National traditions

Experiences

Having different values from others is something we discover as we get older and meet an increasingly wider variety of people outside our own circle of family and close friends.

Activity 4

Look at the three value statements in Source 3.
- How do you feel about the values expressed in each statement?
- What reasons can you give for feeling that way?
- Hold a vote to find out what the majority of people in your class think.

Source 3

1 Food: eating vegetables and not eating meat or animal products is better for everyone.

Source 3 continued

2 Relationships: parents should be able to approve whoever you go out with.

3 Community: senior citizens should always move to the front of the queue.

Activity 5

In London in 2012 seven values were celebrated at the Olympic and Paralympic Games. These were:

| Courage | Determination | Equality | Excellence |

| Friendship | Inspiration | Respect |

Values should influence the way we meet, work and live with others.

Every four years when people from countries across the world come together to compete in the Olympic Games there is a chance for them to share and celebrate their values.

Whatever country they come from, each person is asked to embrace these values, which help nations and competitors to live by a shared set of principles.

Seven values were listed for 2012. **What eighth value would you choose for people to live by and why?** You can only use one word.

Activity 6

What things do you value for yourself? (Examples may include being honest or kind.)

What things do you value for other people? (These are things that may not apply in your life but which you can see have value for others. For example, you may not like sport but can see how being a good sportsman/woman might be important to others.)

2.1 What happens at puberty?

In this lesson you will learn:
- that everyone experiences physical changes as they grow up
- about ways to manage these changes.

Starter

Look at the pictures of the boy and girl in Source 1: they have begun the journey through puberty. What changes might they have experienced?

Use the following three headings to help you think about this:
- Physical – How have their bodies changed?
- Emotional – How have their feelings changed? (Happier? More stressed?)
- Social – How have their relationships with family and friends changed?

 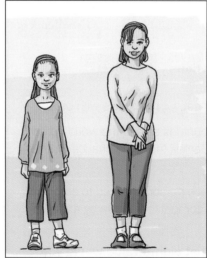

Source 1 Puberty means 'grown-up' or 'adult'. A person going through puberty is experiencing the changes that take them on a journey from being a child to becoming an adult.

When it comes to the word 'puberty', lots of people think it is all about sex. And when it comes to words like 'sex' lots of people get embarrassed. People might use slang, 'dirty words' or family names to describe parts of their bodies. These words might upset some people, and one way to make sure that no one gets upset and that we all understand each other is to agree which words to use.

Activity 1

On page 19 is a list of words for parts of female and male bodies. Copy the diagram of the woman and man in Source 2. Work in pairs and see how many of the parts of the diagram you can label, using the words on page 19.

Female

Clitoris – a small bump about the size of a pea above the urethra. It contains thousands of nerve endings and gives sexual feelings.
Fallopian tube(s) – the egg passes down this towards the uterus
Ovaries – where eggs are produced
Urethra – the opening that urine (wee) comes out of
Uterus/Womb – where a baby grows from a fertilised egg. When an egg is not fertilised, the special lining of the womb is shed each month. This is called 'having a period' (menstruation) and happens from puberty onwards.
Vagina – the opening passage through which menstrual blood passes, in which sexual intercourse takes place and through which a baby is born

Male

Foreskin – a layer of skin covering the end of the penis. Some males have the foreskin removed for health or religious reasons (circumcision).
Penis – the organ that hangs in front of the scrotum. The urethra is a small opening at the tip of the penis.
Scrotum – a sack of soft skin that covers and protects the two testicles
Testicles – in the scrotum and often called 'balls'. They store sperm, which fertilise eggs in the female.
Urethra – the narrow tube inside the penis that carries sperm and urine out of the body

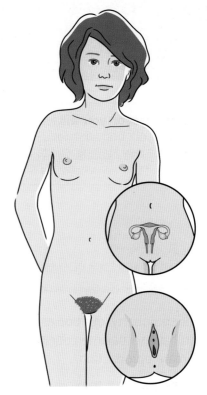

Right now you are aged between eleven and twelve, just like everyone else in your class. If you look around, you will notice that some people are tall, and others are shorter. Some people have big feet and others have small feet. The fact is that puberty happens at different rates and not at exactly the same time for each person. It is natural to worry about feeling different – that you aren't like everyone else seems to be, but at some point everyone will catch up and reach their own adult size.

Activity 2

Think back over all the things you've talked about in this lesson. You may still have questions that you would like answered. On a slip of paper write down one question that you would like to ask privately, fold it up and give it to your teacher. You do not have to write your name next to the question.

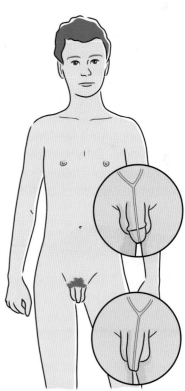

Source 2 Male and female bodies

2.2 How are babies made?

In this lesson you will learn about:
- how your body develops sexual feelings
- how these feelings lead to sexual reproduction
- how fertilisation leads to pregnancy and birth.

Starter

What do you think of when you hear the words 'human reproduction'?

During puberty, our bodies change so that when we are adults we can have sexual intercourse if we want to. Sexual intercourse leads to human reproduction.

Our bodies start to produce hormones that make us feel different from before.

In Year 7 you are too young to have sexual intercourse. The law says a person should only have sex at age sixteen – though that doesn't mean you *have* to!

As people's bodies mature to prepare them for reproduction, they develop sexual feelings. A person might want to touch their genitals because it feels nice and gives them pleasure. This is called masturbation. Different religions and cultures have different attitudes to masturbation. There are lots of myths about it, for example, doing it makes you go blind or stunts your growth. None of these is true.

Activity 1

Human reproduction usually follows the same pattern. Use the cards you will be given. Place them in the right order to describe the sequence that leads up to the birth of a baby.

Some people get embarrassed at even the thought of talking about sex – and yet sex is the most natural thing in the world. Most people's parents have had sexual intercourse – it is how we are made! Sexual intercourse is often called 'making love'. It's a pleasurable feeling so most couples want to do it often. If you want to know more about sex and relationships, then your parents are a good place to start.

Activity 2

What if you are someone who truly feels unable to discuss sex with your parents? Who else could you talk to? Work in pairs to identify a list of adults who you think would be easy to talk to about sex and relationships.

Activity 3

What would you say to a parent who wants to talk to their child about sex and relationships – what advice could you give them?

Nowadays, women can also become pregnant through 'assisted conception', sometimes called 'in vitro' fertilisation. *In vitro* is Latin and means 'in glass'. This is when a woman's egg is fertilised by a sperm outside the human body. This is done with the help of medical experts.

Some people choose to start a family by adopting a baby or child. The new adoptive parent(s) agree to raise the child as their own. They sign an adoption document in front of a lawyer or judge.

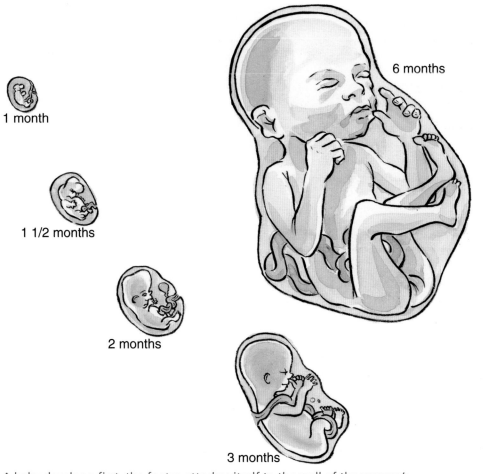

1 month

1 1/2 months

2 months

3 months

6 months

A baby develops: first, the foetus attaches itself to the wall of the woman's uterus. Over the next nine months it grows and develops into a baby.

2.3 What is contraception?

In this lesson you will:
- examine some facts and myths about contraception
- investigate a variety of types of contraception
- consider what advice you could give young people wanting to learn about contraception.

Starter

What do these two words mean?
- Conception
- Contraception

1 The 'pill'	2 'If we do it standing up it'll be fine'	3 IUS
4 'It'll never happen to me'	5 Emergency contraceptive pills	6 'It'll be OK the first time'
7 Contraceptive injection	8 Using clingfilm	9 Pulling out before coming
10 Having sex during a period	11 No sexual intercourse	12 Implant

Source 1 Which of these methods protect against pregnancy?

Activity 1

1 Working with a partner, look at Source 1 above and decide which of these methods protect against pregnancy.
2 Now see if you can match a picture from Source 2 opposite to any of the genuine methods of contraception in Source 1.

Activity 2

Condoms are 98 per cent effective when they are used correctly. This is a really important statement! What are the correct facts about how to use a condom?

Condoms (F in Source 2) work as a simple and effective contraceptive to prevent pregnancy. However, condoms are only really effective if they are used properly. A condom is made of very thin latex (rubber) or polyurethane and fits over a man's erect penis. It acts as a barrier between the man and his partner as it covers the whole of the penis and stops sexual fluids being exchanged. A new condom should be used each time a person has sexual contact.

Before using condoms, it's important to check:
● that the packet has a BSI or CE Kite mark, which shows it's been safety tested
● the instructions in the packet, which have diagrams showing how to use the condoms properly
● the expiry date on the packet.

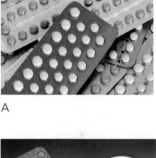
A

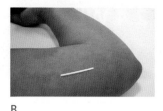
B

C

D

E

F

Source 2 Contraceptives

Activity 3

Roz and Ike are both sixteen. They've been going out for just about a year. They haven't had sex yet – they are thinking about it but have some questions they want answered first. They are planning to go to their local sexual health clinic. Can you help answer their questions?

a) The clinic is a long way from where we live. Can we go to see the doctor instead?

c) Will either of us have to have a physical examination before getting contraception?

Source 3 Roz and Ike

You can check your advice to Roz and Ike against the information at www.brook.org.uk, www.teenagehealthfreak.org or by using leaflets about local health services: these can usually be found in your local library, GP practices, clinics, hospitals, and at young people's services.

b) We've heard that clinics keep things confidential. Is it true that they won't tell anybody else?

d) Are free contraceptives as reliable as the ones you can buy?

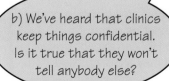
Activity 4

Roz and Ike still have quite a lot to learn and so many things they are worried about. Would it be better for them to wait before having sex?

23

2.4 What are HIV and AIDS?

In this lesson you will:
- learn about the meanings of HIV and AIDS
- research some facts about HIV and AIDS
- discuss how people can be affected by prejudice and how this might be challenged.

Starter

People who have HIV or AIDS sometimes experience a lot of prejudice. Work with another person to:
- think of examples of how these prejudices might be shown
- give reasons why you think this happens.

Human	Only affects people
Immunodeficiency	Stops the immune system working properly
Virus	A living cell that can transmit infections
Acquired	Does not occur naturally – you get it from someone or somewhere else
Immune	The body system that fights illness and infections
Deficiency	Not fully functioning or working
Syndrome	A collection of illnesses or conditions

Source 1

Activity 1

1 Read Source 1 which describes and explains HIV and AIDS and then look at the statements – below.

2 Sort the following statements (a–h) into three groups:
   ✓ True
   ✗ Untrue
   ? Uncertain

   a HIV only affects gay men and people who inject illegal drugs.
   b More than 80,000 people in the UK are living with HIV.
   c You can become infected with HIV if you share food and cutlery with someone who has the virus.
   d The red ribbon is an international symbol of support for people living with HIV and AIDS.
   e HIV is increasing in every region of the world.
   f You cannot get HIV from swimming pools.
   g HIV and AIDS cannot be cured.
   h People living with HIV can expect a near normal life span if they are diagnosed promptly.

Activity 2

There may be some statements from the previous activity that no one is sure about. Use the following websites to do some research.
- www.avert.org/young.htm
- www.cwac.org/education_faq.htm
- www.worldaidsday.org
- www.tht.org.uk

Does your research leave you with any unanswered questions about HIV and AIDS?

In addition to facts and figures about HIV and AIDS, people have also written stories and poems about living with HIV. These tell the human side of the story.

Source 2 is an extract from *Two Weeks with the Queen* by Morris Gleitzman (something you might want to read on your own), which is about a boy called Colin.

In this extract, Colin hears some news about Griff.

Activity 3

Read Source 2 and work in pairs to discuss these questions:
1 Why are some people prejudiced towards those who, like Griff, have HIV or AIDS?
2 How do you think this prejudice makes a person who has HIV or AIDS feel?
3 How does it make others who hear these prejudiced comments feel?
4 What could your class, your school or your community do to try and stop prejudice towards people with HIV and AIDS?

Griff hasn't just got cancer. He's got cancer because he's also got a virus called AIDS.

Colin had heard about that. The government had sent a booklet around about it. He knew it was a virus a lot of people were very scared of …

'Want some?' Griff held out half a tangerine … 'Or would you rather peel your own?'

Colin knew why Griff was giving him the choice. Some people were scared a person with AIDS could give it to you real easy, like a cold or nits. Ted had explained that you could only catch it off stuff from inside the body, blood and stuff like that.

'Thanks,' said Colin. He took half the tangerine.

They talked for ages.

Source 2

Source 3 World AIDS Day

The red ribbon has been an international symbol of HIV for over twenty years. World AIDS Day, 1 December each year, is a chance to show support for the 40 million people living with HIV worldwide.

Many famous people, such as Sir Elton John, work hard to promote HIV and AIDS awareness.

HIV and AIDS affects everyone across the world.

Activity 4

Look at Source 3. What could you do or say if you heard someone making an unkind and prejudiced remark about a person with HIV?

2.5 What are STIs?

In this lesson you will:
- find out about sexually transmitted infections
- learn some facts about condoms.

Starter

How do you think a person could tell whether or not they had a sexually transmitted infection (STI)?

STIs are mainly transmitted (passed from one person to another) during sex. There are at least 25 types of STI with a range of different symptoms.

Activity 1

In pairs decide whether you agree with, disagree with or are not sure about the statements in the STI quiz in Source 1.

Source 1 STI quiz – agree or disagree?

1 You can get STIs from toilet seats.
2 Chlamydia is the most common STI amongst teenagers in the UK.
3 You have to sleep around a lot to get an STI.
4 You always know when you have an STI because it hurts when you pee.
5 All STIs can be cured.
6 You can only have one STI at a time.
7 A person with an STI is only infectious when they have symptoms.
8 STIs can cause infertility.
9 The only way to find out if you have an STI is to get tested.
10 Condoms provide protection against STIs.

Source 2 STI information

Chlamydia
Symptoms: Most people don't have any symptoms for a long time
Effects: Left untreated can cause infertility
Treatment: Antibiotics

Genital warts
Symptoms: Growths or warts in the genital area: they can take a year to appear after infection
Effects: Can be uncomfortable and ugly
Treatment: Ointments or freezing (done by medical professionals)

Herpes
Symptoms: Small painful blisters or sores which heal in a week or two
Effects: Painful when outbreaks of sores occur
Treatment: No cure but tablets and cream can reduce the severity

Pubic lice (or crabs)
Symptoms: Pubic lice are not necessarily sexually transmitted but are usually passed on through close body contact; they can cause severe itching
Effects: No long-term health problems — but will disappear only if treated
Treatment: Special lotions which can be bought in pharmacies

Gonorrhoea
Symptoms: Most women and some men don't have any symptoms
Effects: Left untreated can cause problems including infertility
Treatment: Antibiotics

Syphilis
Symptoms: Sometimes none, sometimes a painless sore may appear within nine to ninety days, followed later by a rash and flu-like symptoms
Effects: If untreated may cause serious permanent health problems such as damage to the nervous system/dementia
Treatment: Antibiotics

Source 2 gives you some information about the six most important STIs to be aware of. These are the ones most likely to be transmitted among young people – and some have serious consequences.

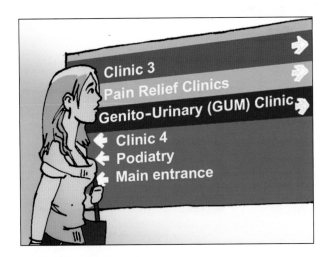

Activity 2

Use the internet, leaflets and local sources of information to find out where, when and how a person in your area could find help and advice about STI worries.

Knowing where your local GUM clinic is could be useful in the future. There is a wide range of free and confidential sexual health advice and contraception services for young people. They may be listed as: genitourinary medicine (GUM) clinics, sexual health clinics or family planning clinics. Brook is a national voluntary sector provider of free and confidential sexual health advice and services specifically for young people under 25.

Three interesting things you might not know about condoms:
- *The ancient Egyptians used a type of condom in 1000BC.*
- *The first advertisement for condoms appeared in 1861 in The New York Times.*
- A Durex condom can hold 40 litres of air, equivalent to 9 gallons of water.

You will probably have learnt about condoms as contraceptives in past lessons – but they are also the most effective barrier against an STI being transmitted between two people.

Activity 3

Think back to what you have learnt about condoms. Name three important things to remember to ensure condoms are used effectively.

Activity 4

Some advertisers find clever and funny slogans to remind us of their products, such as in Source 4. What slogan can you think of to encourage people to use condoms?

Because you're worth it

Melts in your mouth, not in your hands

I'm loving it

Solutions for a smart planet

Source 3 Some advertising slogans

2.6 What does the law say?

In this lesson you will:
- learn about the age of consent
- discover some legal facts about sex.

Starter

Just like many things in life, when it comes to sex, people have to consider their legal position. What is the 'age of consent'?

Activity 1

Look at Source 1. When it comes to understanding the laws about sex, have these young people got their facts right?

Parents have a legal right to withdraw their child from any form of sex and relationship education in school.

It is illegal for a school to teach about homosexuality.

When 14-year-olds go to the young people or family planning services for contraception, their parents/guardians have to be told.

Even if your parents/guardians do not agree, you may get married at 17.

Gay people have an older age of consent than straight people.

You can buy condoms at any age.

If a 15-year-old tells their teacher that they are having a sexual relationship, the teacher has to keep it confidential.

Source 1 Have they got it right?

Activity 2

Read Source 2 and discuss the following questions:

1 Did Jamie break any law:
   a when he sent the photo on to Tom?
   b when he posted it online?

2 Who does sending these 'private' types of photos affect?

3 What can Suzie do?

4 What are the other risks if someone takes 'private' photos and texts them or posts them online?

Suzie and Jamie started going out last year. They were crazy about each other and spent ages on the phone and texting. They'd take selfies blowing kisses to each other and text those too.

A couple of months ago Jamie suggested that they send each other special private pix. Jamie sent a topless one so Suzie copied him and sent one back.

Two weeks ago they split up. Yesterday Tom, Jamie's best mate, stopped Suzie in the street, pointed to her breasts and said, 'Great rack, Suze.'

Suzie thought straight away that Tom must have seen the photo. She went straight round to Jamie's and had a go at him about it. He admitted it but couldn't see why she was so upset. 'It was only a joke! Anyway I put it online two days ago and you didn't say anything then.'

Source 2 Suzie's story

Activity 3

Identify a key fact you have learnt about laws and sexual behaviour.

3.1 Why am I feeling like this?

Starter

1 Can you remember how you felt on the very first day at this school? Were you nervous, excited, worried? Did you know anybody else coming to this school?
2 Compared with then, how have your feelings changed? Why might you feel more relaxed about your school now?

In the previous chapter puberty was discussed from the point of view of the physical changes that take place. But puberty is much more than that. It is the term that describes the changes that take you on a journey from being a child to becoming an adult. These changes include things that happen to our bodies as well as our emotions and our relationships with other people. The hormones that make all the physical changes happen also affect our feelings. We just can't see them!

People are at different places on the journey – some are happy not being too grown-up and others can't wait to be adults. Some are even-tempered while others find their moods change quickly – one minute they're feeling really happy to go along with friends and the next they don't want to talk to anyone!

Dear Problem Page,

I am eleven years old. I started secondary school in September, and I am really unhappy.

My mum and dad split up during the summer holidays. My mum has moved house with me and my sister – we moved from our old town and now we're in this new place.

Most people made friends in primary school and they seem to have lots of friends here at secondary school. I don't know anyone and it's not been easy to make friends. I don't want to bother my mum with this as she's finding it hard enough anyway.

What advice can you give me?

Yours sincerely,
Jenny

Source 1 Problem pages

Dear Problem Page,

I'm thirteen and I've got really bad acne. It feels like everyone's looking at me and I hate it so much that I just want to hide away. I'm sure my friends think I'm the ugliest person in our group. Loads of my friends boast about getting off with someone – I can't. No one would fancy me.

Yours sincerely,
Brian

Dear Problem Page,

On Friday and Saturday nights my friends get to stay out later because they don't have school the next day. My mum and dad won't let me go anywhere, and if I invite friends home I get really embarrassed by them – so I don't ask anyone round. How can I get my parents to treat me like a grown-up?

Yours sincerely,
Hardeep

Source 1 continued Problem pages

Activity 1

Look at Source 1 showing problem page letters from young people of about your age. They all feel that they're facing problems that are part of changing and growing up. Work with a friend to write replies to some of these letters. Imagine that you are an Agony Aunt or Uncle; your job is to give advice, reassurance and sources of help.

Activity 2

Imagine that local secondary schools are contributing to a teenagers' magazine. Your school is focusing on the topic of 'puberty and growing up'. One way of helping people who feel distressed is to give them confidence to do things they will enjoy. Think of ideas for articles to encourage pupils to explore new interests. You might also want to think of people who could be interviewed – especially local people who already work in ways that help and support young people. You and your team need to produce plans for the sort of articles the magazine would feature for Year 7 pupils.

Activity 3

Look at the words in Source 2. They describe some of the emotions that young people feel as they go through all the changes of puberty. Not everyone finds it easy to talk about these emotions. Which two of these emotions might come up most often in young people's conversations? Why did you choose those two emotions? Imagine you could tell advisers on a young people's helpline how to prepare to talk to young people. What would you say?

Source 2

embarrassed   worried   sad   bothered   just OK   different
stupid   bored   amazed   interested   fantastic   nervous
annoyed   scared   curious   angry

3.2 Boys and girls – is there a difference?

In this lesson you will:
- think about whether boys and girls receive equal respect
- consider a range of situations related to gender and stereotypes.

Starter

Are boys and girls treated with equal fairness? Give examples of situations where you think they are and situations where you think they aren't.

Boys and girls are sometimes treated differently from each other, for example, girls are sometimes seen as 'sweet and delicate' and boys as 'rough and tough'. Do you believe this is true? Probably not. But does this attitude affect how boys and girls are treated?

Activity 1

Complete the statement 'If boys and girls treated each other fairly …' with as many endings as you can think of. For example: 'If boys and girls treated each other fairly … then boys would ask before they took over the whole playground for football.'

Think back to when you were younger and played with your own toys. What toys do boys remember playing with and what toys do girls remember playing with? Parents sometimes treat boys and girls differently. They may give toy trucks to boys and give dolls to girls. Parents may get upset if a boy picks up a doll and plays with it because they think a doll is a girl's toy. The same thing might happen when a girl plays with a toy truck or car.

The way the genders treat each other may stem from how parents and other people treat boys and girls differently. Also, girls and boys don't naturally play together when they are young – it takes time to learn to do this.

Activity 2

Work in a small group to discuss and answer these questions, thinking of examples to explain your answers:
1 Do you think boys get less affection at home as they are growing up? For example, are they hugged less just because they are boys?
2 Do parents expect less toughness and ambition from a daughter than they would from a son?

Activity 3

As they grow up boys are often encouraged to be 'macho' in their relationships, while girls in relationships are sometimes criticised for being either 'silly' or 'giggly'. Look at Source 1 and work with others to decide where you stand on these statements. Do you agree or disagree – or are you somewhere in the middle? Whatever your opinion, explain your reasons for your point of view.

Source 1

Do you think it's OK if:

a) men and women are paid differently for doing the same job?

b) a man works as a nursery nurse?

c) a woman is captain of a large aeroplane?

d) a group of girls giggle and point as a cute guy passes by?

e) workmen on a building site whistle and shout 'oi, sexy!' at a woman walking by?

f) a group of young men stare at and follow two young women in the street?

g) a boy walks up behind a girl in school and snaps her bra strap?

h) a male judge in court criticises a female witness for wearing a short skirt and low cut blouse while she gives evidence?

Activity 4

'If you want to be respected by others the great thing is to respect yourself.'

Fedor Dostoevsky

What could you do or say to show that you respect yourself?

3.3 Why are friends important?

In this lesson you will:
- learn that friendships affect everything we do
- understand that positive friendships are important in our lives
- understand that friendships can cause strong feelings and emotions.

Starter

A United States President once said to his friend:

> If we must disagree, let's disagree without being disagreeable.

What do you think he meant?

Activity 1

Today is your opportunity to create an 'I'd be a great friend to have ...' page on an imaginary online site. (Remember it is important to be sensible and safe whenever you are posting personal information online.)

Look at Source 1 and use it to give you some ideas for how to create your personal page. Think carefully about the drawings and phrases you will use to get your message across. Think about your personal characteristics – what are your interests and hobbies, what qualities have you got that make you a great friend?

Friend available

My name is Frankie, I'm twelve and I'm the friendliest, funniest, funkiest mate you could ever hope to have! I like dogs (NOT cats!) and skateboarding, and I'd love to meet other people to share my free time with.

Email me on frankie@me.com. No bores should bother to reply!

Source 1 Friend available

Activity 2

Even the best of friends find that they sometimes disagree or even fall out with each other. Do you think having arguments is a natural part of being friends? What sorts of things do friends argue about? Come up with a list of things that might cause an argument between friends.

Activity 3

Read the following list of situations in which friends might fall out or disagree. Work together with someone and come up with simple suggestions for solving the problem. What would you have to do and what would your friend have to do to keep the friendship going?

- You were invited to spend the night at a friend's house. Half an hour before you were due to leave your friend telephones to cancel. The next day you find out that someone else was invited instead of you.

- You and your friend have decided to join an after-school club. There are two activities that you both want to take part in, however they are both scheduled at the same time.

- For the last couple of months you have been going round to your best friend's house every day after school. You enjoy it but are beginning to feel you'd like to do other things too.

- You and your friend have done something wrong and now your parents have found out. You tell the truth but your friend lies and doesn't admit being involved.

- You've lent a favourite item of clothing to a friend and s/he returns it dirty and with a hole in it.

Source 2 Notes on friendship

The Number One friendship skill is ... being a good listener.

The best thing I can offer another friend is ... my loyalty.

Activity 4

Look at the notes in Source 2 that have been started for you and decide on one thing you would put under each heading.

A best friend would never ... bad mouth me.

We all need friends in life because ... it's good to have someone to play with.

3.4 What are the different types of relationships?

In this lesson you will learn:
- about different types of relationships
- some of the qualities needed to maintain good relationships
- that most relationships go through positive and negative phases and need to be maintained.

Starter

When you hear the expression 'being in a relationship', what do you think of?

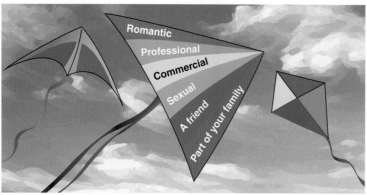

Source 1 Different types of relationships

Source 2 Five qualities

Activity 1

Look at Source 1. Which type of relationship do the following people belong to? Some people could belong to more than one type.

a girl/boyfriend
b step-parent
c shop assistant
d teacher
e aunt/uncle
f doctor (GP)
g neighbour of your age
h bus driver
i person with shared interest, e.g. online gamer
j life partner, husband, wife

Activity 2

Look at Source 2 and the five qualities. Which of these do you think is the most important in maintaining a good relationship?

In any kind of relationship there are qualities that will make the relationship work better for the people involved. For example:
- communication – listening to each other and clearly expressing yourself
- honesty – speaking openly about what is going well or not so well in your relationship.

Source 3 Examples of types of relationships

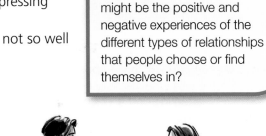

Activity 3

Look at Source 3. What might be the positive and negative experiences of the different types of relationships that people choose or find themselves in?

Going out with your best friend's 'ex'

Being in an arranged relationship/marriage

Living together with step-siblings (step-brothers/sisters)

Having your parent's new partner in the house

Activity 4

Answer this: The best qualities I can bring to one relationship in my life are …?

This lesson has been about different types of relationships and how we try to maintain good relationships. Every relationship will experience its up and downs – life isn't always about having the perfect family and friends, and living happily ever after.

3.5 What do we see about sex in the media?

In this lesson you will learn about:
- some of the ways the media uses sex
- the care needed in using social media
- how pornography affects our lives.

Starter

Think of:
a   an advertisement
b   a music video
c   a TV programme
you have seen which uses 'sexy' images to sell a product or make you want to keep watching.

Activity 1

Look at Source 1. How has sexual imagery been used on this album cover? How do you feel about an image like this being used to sell music?

We live in a society where so much is based around beautiful people in situations suggesting a connection with sex. More and more adverts tell you the perfume or deodorant you use, or the type of car you drive, will make other people fancy you.

Look at music videos and the way people dress, gesture and dance, and the words they sing. They can often give the impression that the only thing young people are interested in is sex.

Switch on the television and join your favourite soap opera characters, who are in relationships with people who aren't their partners, where fourteen-year-olds get pregnant and where no one mentions condoms.

Source 1 Sex sells

Activity 2

Look at Source 2. What problems might this person face from putting this image on their page online? (Don't just think about the present but also the future.) Would sexual images (such as partial nudity, full-on snogging) be more or less of a worry?

When sexual images are used in all sorts of media, it is no wonder that many people start think of seeing such images as normal and ordinary. It's even been suggested that teenagers take this so much for granted that they don't think twice before putting revealing or risky photographs on their social networking pages.

Source 2 A great night out?

Porn is any material (words, sounds, pictures) designed to be sexually arousing. Anatomical pictures may be sexually explicit, but are not intended to be arousing. That's the difference. Pornography has been around for a long time, but what has changed is its accessibility and its content. Your grandparents probably thought of it as top-shelf magazines or under-the-counter videos. In the past, people could see more explicit images more easily – but still not as immediately as at the click of a mouse.

Activity 3

Look at Source 3. In a similar survey of over 400 young people the majority said that adults *should* raise the issue of pornography with them. How would you suggest adults do this?

Seven in 10 school pupils think porn should be taught in sex education classes

"Girls feel they have to look and perform like 'porn stars' to be liked and valued by boys."
CLAIRE LILLEY
POLICY ADVISER AT NSPCC

"More frequently than ever, young people are learning about relationships with others through the internet, including porn and social media"
YAS NECATI
17 YEAR-OLD SCHOOL GIRL SPEARHEADING THE TELEGRAPH CAMPAIGN

Young people are **three times** more likely to go online to find out about sex and relationships than their parents or carers

12% Ask parents

36% Go online

52% Other

28% of school pupils believe pornography dictates how young people have to behave in a relationship

A further 32% say porn "sometimes" affects how young people act when with their partner.

The Telegraph
Better sex ed

Source 3 Pornography survey

Porn influences how we behave. Many images show girls being used just for the enjoyment of others. In reality no woman wants this to happen.

Porn changes how we feel about ourselves and about sex. It's easy to feel inadequate: normal bodies are hairy and wobbly, not super tanned and perfectly toned …

Porn is fantasy. We need to separate out truth (real people) from fantasy (actors).

If watching porn makes you feel weird inside, unhappy, confused or upset – then don't watch it.

Source 4 Adults' worries about pornography

Activity 4

Look at Source 4.
- Are these adults right to be concerned?
- Are these the most important things to be concerned about with pornography?
- Are there other concerns that you would want to discuss?

Activity 5

Think back over this lesson on sex in the media. What key bit of learning would you want to share with a parent of teenagers?

3.6 Is commitment important in relationships?

In this lesson you will:
- think about marriage and stable relationships
- discuss marriage and other partnership ceremonies
- look at the significance of commitment vows.

Starter

The government says it is important for people your age to learn about marriage and stable relationships. Why do you think this was included in a list of topics that schools should cover?

People may feel they are happiest when their lives are stable, when they know they can depend and rely on the people around them. Many people choose to live their lives as part of a couple.

Activity 1

Think about people you see on television or read about in books who live together in couples. Give some examples. For each example, answer the following questions:
1 Why do you think they have chosen to be together?
2 What do you think makes them happier being together than being alone?

When two people live together as discussed in Activity 1, we talk about them having made a 'commitment' to each other. Some people choose to show their commitment to and love for another person by taking part in a ceremony. Marriage and partnership ceremonies are two examples of these as shown in the photos below.

People celebrate their marriages or partnerships by making an act of commitment to each other.

Activity 2

Look at the photos on these two pages and the vows below. List the things that people do in marriage and partnership ceremonies to demonstrate their love and commitment to each other.

Vows are special promises that people make at important times in their lives. At a marriage or partnership ceremony, the two people repeat vows to each other.

For example, in a Christian religious ceremony the two people face each other. One at a time they take each other's hands and say:

> I, … , take you, … ,
> to be my husband/wife,
> to have and to hold
> from this day forward;
> for better, for worse,
> for richer, for poorer,
> in sickness and in health,
> to love and to cherish,
> till death us do part,
> according to God's holy law.
> In the presence of God I make this vow.

Activity 3

Above are the traditional vows people use in a Christian marriage ceremony, but people often write their own vows. Work in pairs to write your own version of a set of marriage or partnership vows. Decide what you think is important for two people to promise to each other.

Activity 4

Just because two people are in a committed relationship doesn't stop things going wrong. Look again at these words:
for better, for worse,
for richer, for poorer,
in sickness and in health
Why should couples think about the ups and downs of being in relationship before they have their ceremony?

Activity 5

Go back to one of the couples you thought about in Activity 1. If you could give them one piece of good advice about marriage or partnership, what would it be?

Signing the register makes the marriage/partnership legal.

Kissing at the wedding ceremony celebrates the couple's happiness.

Many people celebrate their weddings as part of a religious ceremony. This is from a Hindu wedding.

Exchanging rings and making promises to each other form part of most weddings. This is a Jewish 'ketubah' – a marriage contract.

41

3.7 What if I don't want to?

In this lesson you will:
- practise a strategy to help you make choices
- use the strategy to help you advise others
- think about issues surrounding 'early sex'
- learn what 'abuse' is
- consider strategies for dealing with potentially dangerous situations.

Starter

Think back to a time when you were worried about saying 'no' to someone and ended up doing something you didn't want to do. For example, maybe you lent someone your homework to copy.

One of the reasons people often find it hard to say 'no' is because they don't want to hurt the feelings of a person who they care about. This can be particularly true if the other person is someone we feel attracted to and 'fancy' or 'love'. However much we love or care about another person we still have the right to make our own decisions and follow our own choices.

You may already have learnt about the following four steps – they help you choose what's right for you.

How to deal with a risky situation

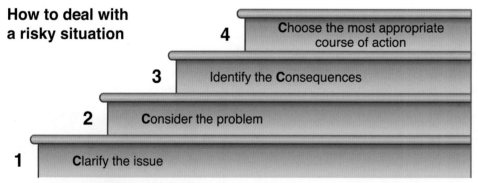

4 **C**hoose the most appropriate course of action

3 Identify the **C**onsequences

2 **C**onsider the problem

1 **C**larify the issue

Source 1 The four Cs

Activity 1

Look at the four situations in Source 2. Choose one situation and use the Four Cs method from Source 1 to help resolve the problem for the main character. If possible, try to achieve a positive outcome for everyone in the situation.

1 Galina

Galina is 15. She has known Si, who's 16 and part of her crowd, for a couple of years. Last time they were all together Si asked her out on her own. Galina was really happy. At the end of the evening Si took Galina back to her house and while they were sitting on the couch he snogged her – it felt brilliant. Si then tried to go further… Galina doesn't want to fall out with him – she's known him ages – but she isn't sure she's ready for this.

2 Hua-Ling

Hua-Ling is 14. She met Zak at the fair and they've been seeing each other for three weeks. He is quite a bit older than her and really good looking – she's the envy of all her friends. Hua-Ling doesn't want to tell Zak how old she is. Zak says that she needs to trust him but she doesn't feel safe being alone with him.

3 Kojo

Kojo met Sandi at the club. They've been together for over a month. The two of them get on really well and Kojo's mates have accepted Sandi as a good friend too. When they've spent time alone there's been a lot of kissing but that's as far as things have gone. Recently Sandi has been suggesting they take things further – but Kojo doesn't feel ready to do this…

4 Rach

Rach is 13 and her parents are letting her have her 14th birthday party at home. They are going out for the evening and leaving Rach's older brothers, Nick and Dan, in charge. A great crowd is coming – and there will be as many boys as girls. The evening goes really well. Nick and Dan are upstairs watching a DVD and downstairs Michael, who really fancies Rach, suggests they go up to her room – no one will notice. Rach fancies him too but this isn't what she wants.

It is natural to want to say 'yes' to somebody to please them. On the other hand, if they care about you, they will understand you have your own feelings and wishes. Looking after yourself and paying attention to your own feelings is not necessarily selfish.

In England the law states people need to be 16 years old before they can choose to have a sexual relationship – not that this means you *have* to have sex when you're 16. Despite all the gossip we might hear and what we read in newspapers and magazines, the majority of young people in this country do wait until they are 16 or older to have sex.

'Early sex' can be defined as having sex before the age of 16 and before a person feels ready to.

Source 3

Activity 2

Imagine two young people like those in Source 3 are trying to decide whether to have or to delay having early sex. What reasons might they come up with in each case?

Activity 3

We all have the right to say 'no'. When saying 'no' to someone you care about, what is important about how you say no?

So far these activities have focused on how to say 'no' to someone you love or care about. However, sometimes other people might try to force you to do things you don't want to do. Or they might lead you towards situations in which you want to please someone, but end up doing something you don't want to do. We call what this other person is doing to you 'abuse'.

WHAT IS 'ABUSE'?

No one has the right to hurt you or make you do anything that feels wrong, but it's not always easy to know if you, or someone you know, is being abused.

Abuse can be many different things: verbal, emotional, physical or sexual. The most important thing to know is that abuse of any kind in any relationship is **never the fault of the person who is being abused**. There are four main kinds of abuse:

Verbal abuse
Someone threatening you or calling you nasty names, for example, someone who shouts at you all the time to make you feel bad.

Emotional abuse
Someone using their power to manipulate and control you. You might feel scared to do something in case it upsets them, or they might constantly check up on you or demand to know where you are all the time.

Physical abuse
Someone physically hurting you in any way (by hitting or slapping you, for example).

Sexual abuse
Someone forcing you into sexual activity you don't want or threatening you if you do not have sexual contact with them (this includes kissing and touching, not just intercourse).

Source 4 What is 'abuse'?

Stranger = danger? Does it?
Many young people have been made aware of the possible danger of strangers. But we know from reports that most abuse is carried out by a family member, a friend or someone the family trusts. If the abuser is not a stranger it may feel even more scary to speak out and say something.

✓ You have the right to be safe. You will not be punished if you tell someone you feel unsafe or threatened in any way by anyone.

✓ You should always seek help if you feel uncomfortable, confused or scared. You will never be blamed for telling the truth.

✓ Your body is your own. Don't let anyone touch you where you don't want to be touched.

✓ Say 'no': you don't have to hug or kiss anyone if you don't want to.

✓ Some secrets should never be kept. Abusers and bullies often say 'it's our secret'. This isn't the truth.

✓ No harm will come to you or your loved ones if you tell the truth about abuse.

Source 5 Personal safety: your rights. Adapted with permission from Brook (www.brook.org.uk/index.php/sex-relationships/harmful-situations/abuse)

Activity 4

Imagine this situation: You are fairly sure, from things they have said and the way they are behaving, that one of your friends is being abused in some way.
- How could you support them in getting the right help?
- What if your friend tells you something bad is happening to them but they think it's their own fault, so they are worried about getting help. What would you say to them?
- They are afraid to even talk much about it because they are afraid of what will happen. Who can you encourage them to talk to without fear or worry?
- Should the police ever be involved?
Use Source 5 to help you support your friend.

Activity 5

A friend asks you to cover for them as they are going to meet someone for the first time and they don't want anyone to know. What's your response?

4.1 What do we mean by 'drugs'?

In this lesson you will learn:
- a definition of the word 'drug'
- some of the risks involved with taking legal drugs.

Starter

What does the word 'drug' mean? Discuss this question and come up with a class definition.

An international definition of the word 'drug' is:
'A substance people take to change the way people feel, think or behave.'

This is the definition of a drug given by the United Nations Office on Drugs and Crime. Is this similar to your class definition? If not, how does it differ? Which definition do you think is better?

You now have a definition of the word 'drug', but what else do you know about drugs?

Activity 1

To make sure we all have some basic information about drugs, answer the following questions in groups then feed back your answers to the rest of the class:

1 What forms could a drug come in?
2 In what ways do people take drugs?
3 What effects do drugs have? How might they change the way a person feels, or thinks or behaves?
4 What legal substances are also drugs? Could medicines be included in this definition?
5 Are tobacco and alcohol also drugs? What is it about them that fits the United Nations' definition above?
6 Do gases, glues and solvents fit the United Nations' definition above? What is it about them that makes them a drug?

It is important not to chase or scare someone who has been using volatile substances.
A sudden change in heart rate – for instance, if they started running away – could be fatal. Can you think of other dangers from using volatile substances?

Legal but dangerous?

In the chart in Source 1 you will find factual information about three drugs. None of these three drugs is illegal, but all of them can be associated with major health problems.

	Alcohol	Tobacco	Volatile substances
What else might it be called?	Booze, drink, bevy	Fags, ciggies, smokes	Glue, aerosols, lighter refills
How would I take it?	As a drink to swallow	Smoked in manufactured cigarettes or hand-rolled; in pipes and cigars	Inhaled (breathed in) through the nose or mouth
If I took it I might feel …	Talkative, happy, friendly or angry, argumentative, dizzy	Able to concentrate more, or relaxed – or dizzy, sick	Silly, dizzy, drunk, argumentative and aggressive
If I use it I might risk …	Being sick (vomiting), having an accident, getting into fights, damaging my liver, doing things I wouldn't normally do	Very lined or wrinkled skin, heart disease, lung infections, cancer	Sickness, blackouts, changing breathing and heart rate, coma

Source 1

Activity 2

Look at the chart in Source 1 and the images on these pages. Choose one key fact about each of the three types of drug (alcohol, tobacco and volatile substances) to feed back to the rest of the class. Your key fact should be what you think is most important to know about the effect of the drug.

It is illegal to sell tobacco products to anyone under the age of 18.

On 6 April 2012, large shops and supermarkets in England were banned from displaying cigarette packets and all tobacco products. What do you think were some of the reasons for introducing the ban?

It may be against the law to drink alcohol in some public places. Do you know if your town or area has rules about this?

Activity 3

Think back over the lesson. Work in pairs to complete this sentence: 'If I were invited back to talk to Year 6 at primary school, the one really important thing I have learnt about drugs that I would tell them is …'

4.2 Drugs – fact or fiction?

In this lesson you will learn:
- what influences your perception of drug use and how this can differ from reality
- some key facts about young people's drug use in the UK.

In the last lesson you learnt what the word 'drug' means. However, many people have different ideas about drugs, and what they think may be influenced by the media.

Starter

Look at the headlines in Source 1 and use them to discuss the following questions:
- Where do people get their ideas and information about drugs?
- What impressions do these headlines give you about drugs?
- Do you think the information about drugs in newspapers and magazines, and on television and the internet is accurate? Give reasons.

Criminal offences by children at 600 a day

Half of all suspects have been using cannabis

Alarming rise in child drug dealers

One in five pupils has tried drugs

Source 1

Activity 1

The media can negatively affect ideas about drug use by what they choose to report and the language they use. For example, the headline: 'Year 7 pupils in our schools regularly drink alcohol!' could be changed to say: 'In a group of 100 pupils in Year 7, 97 do not drink alcohol regularly.'
Both statements are true but they present very different pictures of young people and alcohol use.

1 What message does each of the statements above give about Year 7 pupils drinking alcohol? Discuss how the messages differ.
2 Look again at the headlines in Source 1. Rewrite each one to give the opposite message – by changing negative statements to positive ones.

As we have seen, headlines and reports in the media like those in Source 1 can negatively or positively affect what people think about drugs. Have your thoughts about young people and drug taking been affected by what you have seen, read and heard? Try the quiz in Activity 2 to find out.

Activity 2

Look at the questions below and decide which you think is the correct answer for each one.

Young people and drugs – fact or fiction?

1 In a group of 100 pupils aged eleven how many do not smoke regularly (once a week)?
   a) 99   b) 69   c) 76

2 In a group of 100 pupils aged eleven how many had not drunk alcohol in the last week?
   a) 45   b) 79   c) 99

3 In a group of 100 pupils aged eleven how many had not taken illegal drugs in the last month?
   a) 77   b) 98   c) 55

4 In a group of 100 pupils aged eleven how many had not smoked cannabis during the last year?
   a) 63   b) 49   c) 99

5 In a group of 100 pupils aged twelve how many have never sniffed gases, glues or aerosols?
   a) 56   b) 94   c) 71

6 In a group of 100 pupils aged thirteen how many have never taken an ecstasy tablet?
   a) 47   b) 63   c) 99

Statistics obtained from:
NHS Health and Social Care Information Centre, Public health statistics.
These reports were published between 2005 and 2012.

Activity 3

In pairs, discuss the following question:
Why do we overestimate the numbers of young people who we think are:
● smoking cigarettes
● drinking alcohol
● using illegal drugs?

Not all media is negative. D-World is a good website to find realistic information about health and young people:
www.drugscope-dworld.org.uk

4.3 How do drugs affect people?

In this lesson you will:
- think about the different ways we view people who use drugs
- learn how drugs affect physical, mental and emotional health
- learn that there is help and support available for people who have problems with drugs.

Starter

'Drugs' – what do you think of when you hear that word?
Brainstorm ideas with the rest of the class.

Drugs are all around us. We read about them in newspapers and magazines, see them on TV and hear about them on the news and maybe even from friends. Often, we hear about them in relation to addiction. When you hear somebody described as a drug addict what do you think of?

Activity 1

1 Work together in groups to describe a 'drug addict'. Think about what they look like, where they live, how they spend their time, who their friends are and what drug they take. Now draw an example of one.
2 Feed back and discuss your ideas with the rest of the class.
3 Label your drawing to explain the different effects this drug can have. Source 1 should give you some ideas.
4 Is anybody else affected by your person's drug use? If so, include this in your labelling, explaining how and why they are affected.

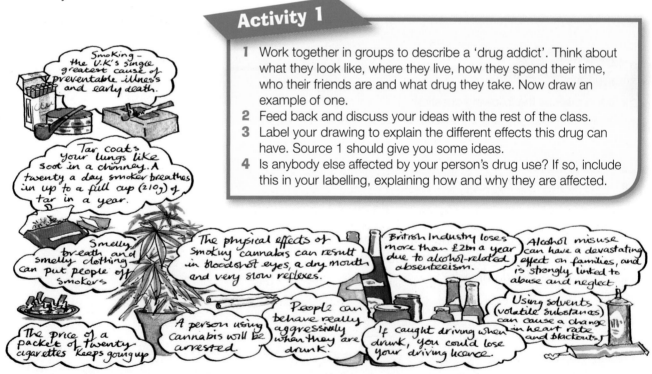

Source 1

Now that you've thought about the ways in which drugs can affect people, let's look at some of the effects of drugs that are commonly used in the UK.

When you thought about drugs did you include:

● tobacco
● alcohol
● medicines
● illegal drugs?

Tobacco and alcohol are the most commonly used drugs in the UK and a lot of people are dependent on them. Most of those people don't enjoy feeling dependent. Feeling a need to have another cigarette or drink to get through the day can make life difficult. That's why a lot of people try to stop, but it isn't easy for them to stop on their own. They need help and support.

Activity 2

Look at Source 2. Read what the man says about giving up smoking and imagine you know someone who is trying to give up. In groups, list three things you could suggest to encourage them.

Tobacco

I was smoking around a pack a day for fifteen years when I decided to give up. I wanted to give up because I hated being dependent on cigarettes and it was becoming socially much more unacceptable to smoke. It was hard as I craved cigarettes all the time for around two months. At the start I avoided being around other smokers so there was no temptation! I then did the 'Stoptober' challenge and after that, it got much easier. Two years on, I love being smoke-free!

Source 2

Alcohol

Think about some popular TV shows (for example, soaps, dramas). Which ones have the characters meeting up in pubs, wine bars and clubs? How realistic is this? Who is drinking alcohol?

Confidential surveys in schools throughout England found that:

● 80 per cent of pupils said they had not drunk any alcohol in the past week. Contrary to media reports, we know that fewer young people aged between eleven and thirteen are drinking alcohol compared to ten years ago.
● In the last ten years, the proportion of pupils who have never drunk alcohol has risen. Most recent statistics say 46 per cent of pupils said they had never had a proper alcoholic drink.
● 65 per cent of the youngest pupils who had drunk alcohol reported drinking it with their parents and relatively few drank alcohol with friends.

Remember, the surveys were confidential so nobody worried that the information could be traced back to them. So, relatively few young people your age drink alcohol. However, as you get older, many of you may find yourselves in situations where alcohol is available. There are some common scenarios on page 52.

Activity 3

Look at the scenarios below and, in groups, answer the questions.

Activity 4

If you wanted to find out more information on alcohol for yourself, a friend or a member of your family, where would you go or who could you talk to?

The group always hung out together in the school holidays. This summer, one or two of them decided they wanted to see what getting drunk felt like. They didn't think they had drunk all that much but suddenly Joe passed out and collapsed on the floor. Nobody knew if it was the alcohol or if something else had gone wrong.

1) What advice would you give the group?
2) What should they do to help Joe?
3) What do you think they should say to Joe's parents?
4) What do you think they should say to their own parents?

Joe

Luci and Rob's dad drinks a lot of alcohol. He often gets very drunk and becomes angry and violent. Sometimes it is so bad he doesn't go to work. Their mum is worried sick about the family and is scared he is going to lose his job. Both the children are worried and want to do something to make things better.

1) What advice would you give Luci and Rob?
2) How could they help their mum?
3) How could they find out where to get help?
4) If the children hadn't talked to each other about their worries, who else could they have talked to?

Luci and Rob

Medicines

People who help you learn about drugs often say, 'All medicines are drugs but not all drugs are medicines.' What is the important point that they are making?

A doctor has to diagnose a person's illness to prescribe the correct medicine – and will take care to prescribe what is suited to the individual. The amount of medicine prescribed for a person will depend on their age, weight, gender and any other medicines they're already taking. This means that medical drugs should be safe as long as you:

● follow the doctor's directions
● listen carefully to what the pharmacist tells you when you collect your medicine
● tell the doctor or pharmacist if the medicine makes you feel strange in any way (side effects)
● don't share the medicine with anyone else, even if they say it's OK – it wasn't prescribed for them, it was prescribed for you.

Sue's mum put some leftover love-heart sweets into an old jar and put them in the kitchen cupboard, telling Sue not to touch them.

Later on, Gran was having trouble opening the cap on her pill bottle, so she found an empty cake sprinkles pot to put them in. She put the pot at the back of the kitchen cupboard because she knew no one would look for them there.

In the evening, Dad put some leftover slug pellets in a jar and labelled it. He put the jar in the kitchen cupboard where all the jars live.

After dinner, while everyone was watching TV, Sue got a stool, climbed up to the cupboard, took down the love hearts, ate a few and put the rest back. Her little brother Tom was watching. He knew she was being naughty but he wanted to eat sweets too. When she left he copied her with the stool, found the love hearts and ate them all. He looked around in the cupboard for more sweets to eat.

Source 3 What could go wrong?

Illegal drugs

Drug use can never be 100 per cent safe. Even legal drugs may have side effects, or people may have allergic reactions to them, or accidentally overdose on them. Using illegal drugs has additional risks.

Illegal drugs are not made in medically controlled conditions, so people can't be sure what's in them. Drug suppliers aren't interested in you having a good time – they just want to make as much money as possible.

Activity 5

A sensible adult will know not to take someone else's prescribed medicine, but there should be some basic rules about medicines in any home to keep children safe too.

Read Source 3. What are the dangers here? Create a list of rules that you think Sue's family should put in place to avoid people being harmed.

FRANK is the National Drugs Helpline: **0300 123 6600**
If you want to talk, you can call FRANK free, 24 hours a day, 365 days a year.

Activity 6

If a person uses illegal drugs and becomes dependent on them, what impact might this have on their:
- health
- employment
- family
- friends
- education
- neighbourhood
- travel
- freedom?

Activity 7

Give one reason to explain why talking about 'drug dependency' is more helpful than talking about 'drug addiction'.

4.4 What about drugs and the law?

In this lesson you will:
- find out about the Misuse of Drugs Act
- identify situations where people may be breaking the law.

Amphetamines

Starter

Think back over what you have already learnt about drugs in your lessons. Work in pairs to come up with two important facts that you have learnt.

Cannabis

The likelihood is that you will have remembered a lot about the harm dugs can cause – but it's important to remember that some drugs are very helpful.

When drugs are licensed to be used as medicines in this country they have been through a series of trials to try to make sure they are as safe as possible.

Cocaine and crack cocaine

You will now realise that taking any drug (even medicines) may cause problems. For that reason society gives careful thought to the way it allows drugs to be used.

There is a law called the Misuse of Drugs Act which classifies drugs into three groups. These groups are Class A, Class B and Class C. Each class carries different legal penalties for having the drugs or for selling them/giving them away.

Activity 1

Name one rule about drugs in your school. (Remember 'drugs' refers to all drugs including medicines, volatile substances/solvents, alcohol, tobacco and illegal drugs.) Why do you think the school introduced this rule?

Activity 2

The photos on page 55 show a variety of drugs that are covered by the Misuse of Drugs Act. Look at Source 1 and decide which class you think each drug belongs in.

Ecstasy

Heroin

LSD

Class	Maximum penalty for possession (having them)	Maximum penalty for supplying (selling or giving them away)
A	Up to seven years in prison or an unlimited fine or both	Up to life in prison or an unlimited fine or both
B	Up to five years in prison or an unlimited fine or both	Up to fourteen years in prison or an unlimited fine or both
C	Up to two years in prison or an unlimited fine or both	Up to fourteen years in prison or an unlimited fine or both

Source 1 The Misuse of Drugs Act – maximum penalties

Magic mushrooms

The Misuse of Drugs Act does not cover all drugs. The Medicines Act covers the use and supply of medicines and there are other laws that control the use and supply of alcohol, tobacco and solvents.

Activity 3

In each of the following situations is anyone breaking the law? If so, identify who is breaking the law and how.
- Pat and Chris are fourteen. They are drinking cider on a street corner.
- Pradip is sixteen. He goes into Mrs Smith's shop and buys cigarettes from her.
- Danni is fifteen. She is with her friends in the shopping centre. She has some cannabis in her bag.
- Aasif and Dayo are sitting in the park sniffing solvents.
- Lou is at a party and gives Jan an ecstasy tablet which she accepts.

Tranquillisers

Activity 4

Laws and facts about drugs are fairly complicated. There is a lot of misinformation and misunderstanding. Identify one new thing you have learnt today. How could it help you and your friends?

4.5 How do I manage situations involving drugs?

In this lesson you will:
- consider different ways of looking at 'risk'
- find ways to keep yourself and others safe
- reflect on the impact of risk taking with drugs.

What is risk?

Risk is the chance that harm might be caused. When we think about risk we need to think about two things:

1 the *what* – the harms that might happen to us
2 the *might* – the likelihood that harm will happen to us.

Take, for example, the risk of a bungee rope snapping. The chance of being harmed if the rope snaps mid-jump is high, but the likelihood of this happening is low. Bungee jumping is highly regulated, there are many safety tests, and, considering the number of jumps each day, the actual risk is of 1 in 500,000 jumps being fatal.

Starter

What events can you think of where drugs being present could lead to risky situations occurring? Think of one example for each of the following:
- medicines
- alcohol
- solvents
- illegal drugs.

Taking drugs is never risk free and different situations will present different levels of risk. Social situations may be risky because sometimes we leave it up to our friends to do the thinking for us.

Activity 1

Look at Source 1. Working in pairs, come up with ideas about what is going on in the story. At first glance does it look as if any of the main characters are involved in risky behaviours? If so, what might they be?

Activity 3

Imagine you could sit down with one of the characters from the story and offer them a piece of good advice. What would it be?

Activity 2

Think about the issues of risk and safety at the party in Source 1. In pairs, list the risks taken and then try to group them into different types of risk. For example, risks to health.

Chantelle is invited with Mark, Surina and Rash to Jade's fifteenth birthday party.

Jade's parents leave her older brother and sister in charge.

Mark buys some cigarettes.

At the off licence…

Rash tells them what he thinks.

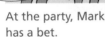

At the party, Mark has a bet.

There are lots of drinks to choose from.

Chantelle has to decide.

The party is underway.

Some older guys chat them up.

Chantelle feels faint.

Source 1 Chantelle, Mark and their friends – the party.
Party scenario adapted for use from the Home Office's Blueprint programme Teacher Manual, Spring 2005.

How will Chantelle get home?

Source 2

Bungee jumping

Parkour

Texting to ask someone out on a date

Speaking in front of your class

Activity 4

Look at Source 2. For each of these situations answer the following questions:
1 Are there risks involved?
2 If there are risks, what are they?

Sometimes people take risks because they know or believe that the benefits they may possibly gain would outweigh any possible negative results. You could call this 'risking on purpose'. At times people do things on the spur of the moment without thinking through what might happen. They may be taking an 'unconsidered risk'.

Activity 5

Now think about different drugs and why they might involve risks. Here are five statements designed to test your awareness on the topic of drugs and risks. Decide whether you think each statement is true or false.
1 Smoking only a few cigarettes a day is fine.
2 Alcohol slows down the brain.
3 Giving your own prescription medicines to someone else isn't a problem.
4 At least one young person a month dies from sniffing solvents.
5 You could be sent to prison for five years for being found with cannabis.

Despite all the information we have about drugs, people still take risks.

Different people have different reasons for taking risks with drugs. Here are some of the reasons people give:

- curiosity
- for a dare
- because they like the feeling
- to show off
- boredom
- to help someone
- because they are influenced by someone else.

Activity 6

Look at the drugs listed in Source 3 and rank them on the ladder with the one you think has the highest risk at the top and the one you think has the lowest risk at the bottom. Be ready to explain your decisions.

Source 3

Alcohol
Amphetamines
Caffeine
Cannabis
Cocaine
Ecstasy
Heroin
Medicines – prescription
Medicines – shop-bought
Poppers
Solvents
Tobacco

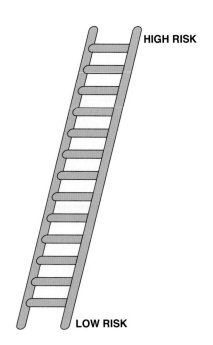

HIGH RISK

LOW RISK

Activity 7

You started the lesson on drugs and the law by identifying two important facts. Now identify something new that you have learnt in *this* lesson about drugs and risk.

5.1 What am I good at?

Starter

'You can't judge a book by its cover.' What do you think this means? If you could choose your own personal qualities, for example being friendly, cheerful, adventurous, sensitive, what would you choose? Take a few minutes to think about this and come up with three qualities that you would like to have.

Activity 1

Now that you've had the chance to think about the qualities you *wish* you had, here's an opportunity to hear about the positive qualities your classmates *know* you have.

Working in groups, look at Source 1. Select examples of the positive qualities that you see in each other (or your teacher will hand out cards for you to give each other).

Give your reasons for selecting these qualities – and invent extra ones if you wish.

fun   sensible   happy   hard-working   tries hard   likable   confident   quiet   friendly   careful

sociable   loyal   thoughtful   warm-hearted   considerate   trustworthy   generous   kind   humorous

responsible   honest   popular   cheerful   good listener   brave   fair   intelligent   polite

bright   reasonable   helpful   capable   great sense of humour   laid back   tolerant   reliable

amiable   tenacious   calm   considerate

Source 1 Positive qualities

Hopefully by now you will have begun to recognise that you are unique. Even though everyone in the class is in the same year group, and you are all around the same age, you are all different. You have special characteristics, talents and abilities that make you who you are.

We all have 'off-days' when perhaps we don't feel happy, can't seem to do anything right, get into arguments, or maybe even break things by accident. Nobody knows why this happens, but it does, and it happens no matter how young or old we are. It's at times like these that we need to know that we are still worthwhile – knowing that our peers think we are OK really helps.

Activity 2

Here you have the opportunity to think about what your classmates are good at – and to tell them. In groups of six, each write your name at the head of a page and pass the paper to the person on your left. Each person writes a skill particular to the person named, folds the paper and passes it on.

Are you surprised by the skills that have been listed for you?

Source 2 Feeling like me

Activity 3

By now you will have begun to realise that you are valued by other people. You and other members of the class have identified several of your positive attributes and you will have done the same for them. But even with all this positive feedback nobody actually knows how it feels to be you.

Look at Source 2. These are artists' examples of self-expression. On a plain sheet of paper make a picture of what it feels like to be you. You don't have to be brilliant at drawing – you can use lines, shapes and colours to express how you feel and a few words too if that helps. What you do is up to you!

Activity 4

How would you want to finish this sentence?
'I believe I am unique, and people in this class have recognised that I am skilled at …'
On your picture from Activity 3 write your completed sentence.

5.2 What does 'assertiveness' mean?

In this lesson you will learn:
- about the meaning of 'being assertive'
- the difference between being assertive and being aggressive
- to practise assertiveness skills.

Starter

Think of as many different ways as you can to say the word 'yes', so that each time it has a different meaning.
Try saying it to yourself in your head as if you …
- really, really mean it
- are not sure if you mean it
- don't mean it at all.

Try out these different ways of saying 'yes' with a partner, but don't reveal which is which. Could they guess the different feelings or thoughts you were having as you said each one? How could they tell?

Are there any other ways of saying 'yes' which people use when they might not mean it? For example, saying 'yes' but with such a big sigh that the other person knows you think it's a real hassle and you don't want to do it.

Our tone of voice, the expressions we use, the speed at which we speak – all of these affect how our words are heard. The way we say words can reveal different feelings or thoughts.

As with 'yes', the way we say 'no' to something can reveal our true feelings. Here are some words that describe different ways of saying 'no':

timidly	ferociously	calmly	gently
aggressively	assertively	sweetly	

Let's take two of these words that people sometimes mistake for each other: 'aggressively' and 'assertively'. Here are some definitions to explain the difference:

Speaking aggressively:	**attacking**
	being hostile
	being offensive
Speaking assertively:	**declaring**
	being confident
	being sure

Activity 1

Working together in small groups, make notes to answer and report back on these questions:

- Are there other ways you could explain the difference between these two ways of speaking?
- What could be the result of an individual/group/nation speaking to another individual/group/nation aggressively?
- Why could being assertive be a better way of dealing with a problem than being aggressive?

How to be assertive – some tips

- Be sure you know what you want.
- Sit or stand up straight – your body language should be relaxed but not casual.
- Use a serious expression – match your expression to the words you use – look like you mean it!
- Look directly at the person you are talking to.
- Use a clear, firm voice.
- Say what you want or need.
- Listen to the other person.
- Repeat your message as often as you need to.
- Suggest alternatives that are acceptable to you – this could show you still want to be friendly with the other person even if you can't at first agree.

Source 1

Activity 2

Speaking assertively isn't always easy – especially when people put pressure on us to agree with them, when we might have a different point of view or we want to say 'no'. Look at the list of tips for being assertive in Source 1. What do you think of them? Would they help you to be assertive without becoming aggressive? Why?

Activity 3

Your teacher will give you a scenario card that describes a situation in which the most sensible course of action would be to refuse to go along with the suggestion.

Look at Source 2. One person is trying to persuade the other. Work together in a pair to role play the conversation. In the first scenario person A acts as the 'persuader' and B as the 'asserter'; then A and B can swap roles or try another scenario card.

After you have role played the conversation both ways, give your partner feedback on the good things they did to demonstrate they could be assertive without being aggressive.

Source 2 Persuasion and assertion

Activity 4

Look back over the different scenarios described in Activity 3 where someone might need to be assertive. Can you suggest another scenario where this might be helpful?

In this lesson you will:
- learn how our mental and emotional health affect our ability to lead fulfilling lives
- learn that there is help and support available when our mental and emotional health is threatened
- find out how and when to get help.

Starter

Sometimes things build up inside us so much that we think we might explode! Imagine blowing air into a balloon until that point where the air pressure inside is so great that the balloon can't take any more. You can let the air out of a balloon to reduce the pressure. What can a person do to reduce the pressure on them and let their feelings out? Work in pairs to come up with some examples.

What does mental health mean? The charity Mind explains it like this:

The word 'mental' means 'of the mind': your thoughts, feelings and understanding of yourself and the world around you. The word 'health' generally describes the working order of your body and mind. So when we talk about 'mental health' we are referring to the working order of your mind.

Sometimes things go wrong with our bodies. We may become ill or get hurt in an accident. In the same way, if something upsetting or tragic happens in our lives, or we simply feel low or depressed, we may have problems with our mental health.

Activity 1

There's a big range of things that people might experience when their mental health is under pressure. For example, a person might feel very sad and want to cry, or perhaps think it's not worth getting out of bed in the morning. These feeling are perfectly natural and do not necessarily mean that someone is suffering mental ill health – but if those things continue, and build up, then there might be a problem. In groups, discuss and come up with other examples of the way mental ill health might show itself in people.

Joe's story

Joe had been off school for quite a while because he had to have an operation. While he was at home recovering, the family received some sad news – his grandma, who lived abroad, had died. Joe was sad that he would not see her again and knew that both his parents were really upset as well. When he got back to school he was disappointed to find that his doctor wouldn't let him take part in any PE lessons – and even worse he couldn't play football so that meant he was no longer part of the school team. To cap it all, Mark, his best friend, announced he would be moving away at the end of term because his mother had a new job in another town. Joe began to feel really depressed. He didn't look forward to going to school and he felt sad when he was at home. It seemed that everything he was used to was changing. His friends noticed he was becoming very quiet and keeping himself to himself.

Picture posed by model

Source 1

Activity 2

Read Source 1 and work in pairs to discuss these questions:
1 Do you think Joe's feelings are a normal response to his situation?
2 Mark wants to support Joe but isn't sure how to start a conversation. How would you advise Mark to begin?
3 Who could Joe (or even Mark, on his behalf) turn to for help and advice?

It is natural to want help from other people when we experience difficult feelings and problems. But there are some things we can do to boost our own mental health (see Source 2).

Activity 3

1 Look at the list in Source 2 and discuss why each item might help someone's emotional wellbeing.
2 Can you think of anything else that helps our emotional and mental health? Make a list of your ideas.

Activity 4

How easy do you think it would be for someone in your school who was feeling down to be able to say so and ask for help? Give some reasons to explain your answer.

From time to time we all need help from other people with our feelings and problems. If you are worried, cross or sad then talk to someone you trust. You can also call Childline free on 0800 1111, or Samaritans on 08457 90 90 90, or you can look up their local numbers.

☐ Remember times when you felt safe and looked after.

☐ Make sure you get enough sleep.

☐ Try to eat healthily.

☐ Get enough exercise you enjoy, for example, swimming, skating, cycling.

☐ Spend time caring for something or someone else, for example looking after a pet, or helping a neighbour.

☐ Talk to someone who you feel close to.

☐ Spend time with good friends who are helpful and look out for you.

Source 2 Looking after yourself

5.4 What does 'resilience' mean?

In this lesson you will:
- recognise that the way in which you see your personal qualities, attitudes, skills and achievements affects your confidence and self-esteem
- reflect on your own personal strengths and achievements
- learn about resilience and how it can help you.

Starter

Young people find it really easy to list all their faults and failings but they often find it difficult to see their good points. Working in pairs, take turns to tell your partner one thing about yourself that is good or positive.

Your partner may have used one of the words in Source 1. These are words that could be used when talking about yourself or others in a positive way.

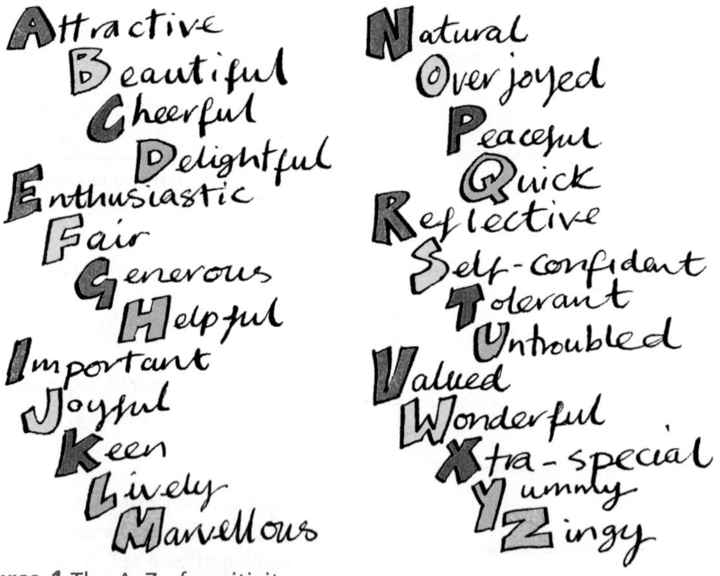

Attractive
Beautiful
Cheerful
Delightful
Enthusiastic
Fair
Generous
Helpful
Important
Joyful
Keen
Lively
Marvellous
Natural
Overjoyed
Peaceful
Quick
Reflective
Self-confident
Tolerant
Untroubled
Valued
Wonderful
Xtra-special
Yummy
Zingy

Source 1 The A–Z of positivity

Activity 1

1. Look at the list of words in Source 1. Choose three different words that match three letters in your name.
2. Work on your own to explain what each of the three words means and then try to think of a word that means the opposite of each.

There are two ways to balance the times when we are negative about ourselves. The first is to think about positive ways to describe ourselves. The second is being honest about our positive qualities – don't be too shy to say when you are good at something.
The game in Activity 2 relies on you being honest and positive.

Activity 2

Your teacher will give you some cards. Place the pile upside down in the centre of your group. Listen carefully to the instructions on how to play the game. You are free to pass *once* if you can't think how to complete the sentence on the card or you may ask other group members to help you.

If you have a positive attitude you are more likely to feel better about yourself and about life in general. Look at Source 2. Here are two statements that somebody could have made about the same situation:

Source 2 Resilience

Another way of being resilient is to use sayings to help you see the positive side of life. Look at Source 3.

Source 3 Resilience sayings

A definition of resilience could be: 'a set of qualities that helps a person cope with the negative feelings that happen when things go wrong for them'.

Activity 3

The sayings in Source 3 are great for helping an individual to become more resilient and get a positive outlook on life. However, sometimes a whole group can become negative. Some members of a group can bring each other down, even when they don't mean to.

As a class, discuss and come up with some mottos or sayings that could help your class stay positive.

Activity 4

Is there a situation that you can remember when you did not feel positive about yourself? How could you look at it now in a more positive way?

5.5 Is anybody perfect?

In this lesson you will:
- look at how the way you see and feel about yourself is affected by a range of factors
- look at differences between people and explore what 'empathy' means.

Starter

If you were asked to bring your favourite photograph of yourself into school, which one would it be? Describe it. For example:
- What are you doing?
- Is anyone else in it?
- Where was it taken?

The photographs and images we see in the media are usually of 'perfect' or 'beautiful' people. But there is also the saying that 'Beauty is in the eye of the beholder'. For example, look at the images in Source 1. Each shows an image which different cultures and tastes would find beautiful.

Activity 1

As a class, discuss the following questions:
1. Why do you think that the media usually shows 'perfect' or 'beautiful' people?
2. What do you think 'Beauty is in the eye of the beholder' means? Use the images in Source 1 in your discussion.

Source 1 Different kinds of beauty

Activity 2

When talking about how people look and feel, the expression 'body image' is often used. What does it really mean?
Work in small groups to come up with some ideas of what 'body image' means to you.

People's body image is often influenced by the way others react to them. Different types of body sometimes attract attention and comment from others, which aren't always positive. Comments can sometimes be cruel but more often they are likely to be just thoughtless. When someone stops and imagines what it feels like to 'live in someone else's skin' they may be more considerate of the other person's feelings. We call this way of identifying with someone else's situation 'empathy'.

Activity 3

Work in pairs to write an empathetic response to the problem page letters in Source 2.
Some good points in helping to express empathy:
- Try to avoid saying 'I know what it feels like … '
  – everyone feels different.
- Be supportive in what you say rather than telling them what to do.
- If you can think of people or services that could offer help, you might want to mention them.

Dear Problem Page

All my friends are allowed to wear make-up at weekends when we go out. They are experimenting with different types of lipstick and mascara. My family think make-up is not necessary for anyone and certainly won't let me use it. They are so old-fashioned! They might as well live on a different planet. I think I look awful without make-up and I want to keep in with my friends.

What should I do?

A. F.

Dear Problem Page

During a sports event, I fell and broke one of my front teeth. The dentist has said I cannot have a crown on it until I am at least sixteen because my mouth is still growing and changing. I am so embarrassed and won't open my mouth to smile any more in case people laugh. I really hate how this makes me look.

What can I do?

B. T.

Source 2 Problem page letters

Activity 4

From what you have learnt in today's lesson, can you identify anything new about the way you might:
- look at yourself
- view others?

5.6 How do I manage my feelings?

Starter

Read Source 1 and think about all the different emotions Fraser might have felt from the moment he woke up that morning to the start of his maths lesson. List as many feelings as you can.

Source 1 Fraser's story

Fraser is fifteen years old and lives with his mum. This morning at breakfast she checked he'd done all his homework because recently he'd been late with several assignments. His mum soon realised that Fraser had not completed his maths homework. She was absolutely furious. Fraser had never heard her shout so much. She made him sit down and do it at the breakfast table.

Fraser left for school and asked his best mate Simon if he could see his homework. Simon said, 'No, you're always borrowing it.'

At school he saw Sindy and asked her the same question. Sindy showed him her homework and they compared their answers, which were virtually the same.

Fraser and Sindy made their way to the maths lesson and found a supply teacher standing in the room – their usual teacher was off sick.

If a relationship is important to us it creates in us all sorts of strong feelings – both positive and negative. In Fraser's case while he knows his mum really loves him he felt very hurt and upset when she lost her temper with him. These strong feelings apply whether the relationship is within your family or with friends: when someone is important to you, feelings matter.

Activity 1

What feelings have you experienced over friendships you've had in your life? Look at Source 2 and write down those you have experienced.

happy   jealous   excited

worried   ANTICIPATORY   embarrassed

reassured   Spiteful   APPRECIATED

loved   faithful   relaxed   loyal

respected   impressed

sociable   fantastic   outraged

TRUSTED   threatened   PRESSURED

RIDICULED   reliable   UNWANTED

criticised   irrepressible   irritated

competitive   ignored   carefree

Source 2 Feelings

Although we all experience a range of emotions it does sometimes feel as if they are happening to us and we are not in control of our feelings. When this happens it can be tempting to blame other people for how we feel. Blaming other people doesn't actually change anything – what we need to do is deal with our feelings in positive ways that help us get back on track.

David Weir, CBE: Paralympic Gold Medallist

'I was born with something called a spinal cord transection. My spinal cord was severed. I've got some feeling in my lower half, but cannot lock my legs or stand up at all.

My parents never treated me like I was disabled or different in any way. As a kid, I'd give anything a go. I was allowed to climb trees on the estate. I loved football and boxing but I couldn't do them. I had to find something I could do in a chair. I got into wheelchair basketball but I didn't get far because there weren't any teams near me.

I remember watching the London Marathon wheelchair race and thinking: 'I want to try that'. I entered the London mini-marathon. I was eight. I didn't have a racing wheelchair so I raced in a standard day chair. I think I impressed everyone, including myself, with how well I did. I'd found my sport. From that point on, there was no looking back.

My first Games were in Atlanta in 1996. I went there as a 17-year-old expecting a wow factor but I didn't get it. I fell out of love with the sport and when I got back I just didn't want to do it anymore.

I was sitting on the sofa watching Tanni Grey-Thompson winning all her medals at the Sydney Paralympics in 2000. I regretted every minute of my four-year break from the sport. I wished I was there. I may have been in medal contention, you never know. That experience just drove me on. It renewed my desire to represent my country again and win gold medals.'

Source 3 Case study
From www.nhs.uk/Livewell/fitness/Pages/david-weir-paralympics.aspx

Source 4 Case study
Extract from *Conversations with Maya Angelou* by Jeffrey Elliot

Professor Maya Angelou

Maya Angelou was a writer and poet. Her most famous book is *I Know Why the Caged Bird Sings*.

In an interview Angelou talked about being black and female and six feet tall when she would rather have been 'pretty' or petite because 'everyone seemed to love those girls'. She talked about how she overcame her negative feelings:

If you're black and every model of beauty is either white or dark-skinned black, then it has to create some insecurity in a person like me, who couldn't possibly conform …

I reached into my race memories to find those positive things that I could use to help myself and raise my son. I rejected those things that were negative; and not just the negative from the white community,
but the negative from the black community as well.
I still reject both of them. I want no part of them …

One of the first things that a young person must internalise, deep down in the blood and bones, is the understanding that although he may encounter many defeats, he must not be defeated …

Look at a diamond: it is the result of extreme pressure. Less pressure, it is crystal; less than that, it's coal; and less than that, it is fossilised leaves or just plain dirt.

Activity 2

Read the case studies in Sources 3 and 4.
1   What experiences are the speakers describing that could have left them feeling they didn't fit in?
2   What ideas and thoughts did they have and how did they behave to help them overcome the difficulties they faced?
3   'You may not control all the events that happen to you, but you can decide not to be reduced by them.' How does this quote by Maya Angelou apply to both of the people you've just read about?

What is resilience?

Why is it that some people bounce back after being hit by life's problems, while others find it hard to pick themselves up off the floor? Think back to some of the big challenges in your life: your first day at school; making friends; your performance for the sports team; your role in the Christmas pantomime; sitting tests and exams; moving up to secondary school. We've all made mistakes in some or all of these areas, but those who bounce back, dust themselves off and start all over again are the ones with resilience.

Taking an exam

Activity 3

Look at the example in Source 5. It shows how one person rates their own resilience. For example, they think they are not good at staying positive and optimistic but they do feel able to talk and seek help. Construct your own chart or table which helps you recognise how resilient you are.

Source 5 How resilient am I?

When things go wrong I ...	Not great	OK	Good	Excellent
take personal responsibility		✔		
am skilled at solving my own problems			✔	
stay positive and optimistic	✔			
am able to talk about it and seek help			✔	

Activity 4

If you were to develop one new coping strategy that would enable you to build up your resilience what would it be?

5.7 What happens when relationships break down?

In this lesson you will:
- understand that all families experience highs and lows
- consider strategies for coping when there are family arguments
- look at some of the issues affecting young people in troubled families.

Source 1 Extract from 'It's All Relative' by Patrick Tolan

Family should mean that arguments can be forgotten
Family should be there when you're feeling downtrodden
Mothers should kiss the wounds that life deals
Fathers should offer advice like no other man can …
Unfortunately families, like most ideals, are never truly perfected
But this brute fact is not a curse but a blessing
We need our families to be imperfect, that we may experience but a small part of the conflict the world bears
So families need not be any of these things, all they need be …
… Is Family

Starter

Read Source 1. Everyone probably wishes they had the perfect family, but the poet in Source 1 recognises that there is no such thing as perfection where families are concerned. What things happen in reality that can cause problems in family life?

Parents have the right to expect you to behave yourself, do your homework and do your jobs around the house. Not getting the latest designer gear isn't being bullied or neglected!

Sometimes the normal rows between siblings and other family members get heavy. People around you may think your feelings don't need to be taken seriously. They may have so much on their minds they can't see your problem.

Activity 1

1. Look at Source 2. What do you think the young person is:
   - feeling
   - thinking?
2. What strategies could you suggest to them to help them cope with what is going on?

Source 2 When it all gets too much

For some people problems become too complicated for them to deal with on their own. Their best move is to tell a teacher or some other adult they like and trust, or to ring Childline on 0800 1111.

Sometimes relationships between the parents in a family break down so irretrievably that they decide to split up. Nothing prepares a young person for this. Even if they are used to hearing their parents rowing or seeing them ignoring each other, it still comes as a big shock.

The young person may feel totally confused, or it could be a relief if their parents' marriage had been very unhappy. Whatever the cause of the break-up, it is not the young person's fault. They did not cause it and they cannot mend it.

Alex

Alex is aware of the difficulties in his parents' marriage. Both of Alex's parents are unhappy and all their attention and time seems to be spent on dealing with the problems between them. Alex is feeling very distressed, full of negative feelings and fears that need to be expressed, but he is worried that his parents have enough to cope with.

Source 3

Within any relationship, there are ups and downs – people say and do things to each other that are hurtful. However, there's a difference between a normal argument and abusive, violent or threatening behaviour. Sometimes disagreements at home turn from arguments to attacks – verbal or physical. This is sometimes referred to as domestic violence or domestic abuse. It can take many forms.

If you are worried about domestic abuse (for yourself or for someone else) you might find it helpful to talk to another adult or one of your teachers about this. Alternatively you can read more and find further help at www.thehideout.org.uk.

Experiencing ups and downs in family life is normal.
Remember: despite what we might see on television or read about in newspapers, the problems in most families do not involve abuse or violence.

Activity 2

Read Source 3. What advice can you give Alex? Write a script where Alex starts a conversation with his mum and dad. Try to find words that express Alex's feelings.

Activity 3

Read the Information Sheet that your teacher will give you. In pairs, create an A5 flier called 'Personal help and information' with three key messages to encourage and support a young person who may be experiencing domestic violence in their home.

Activity 4

This lesson began with a poem. Write your own three-line poem (it can be a haiku) that expresses something positive about your family or a family member.

5.8 How do we cope with loss and bereavement?

In this lesson you will:
- explore what 'loss' and 'bereavement' might mean
- consider ways that people may cope with loss
- discuss different ways of dealing with death.

Starter

When we hear the phrase 'loss and bereavement' many of us naturally think first of death – either of someone we love or of someone we know who is feeling grief because someone they love has died.
What other events in our lives might make us feel a sense of loss and painful sadness at missing someone or something?

By your age you will have experienced a range of different types of relationships in your life: a best friend or friends; a very close group of friends that you hang out with; long-standing friends from aspects of your life not connected with school; perhaps a boyfriend or girlfriend. Sometimes those relationships can break down or end suddenly. When this happens you may feel rejected, or sad, or that you don't ever feel you can trust anyone again.

Source 1 Anya's feelings

I'm going to be 16 next term. Three months ago Daniel, who I'd been going out with for over a year, suddenly said he was ending our relationship. He didn't give a reason, he just wanted out. The trouble is, I just can't seem to get over him. I think of Daniel all the time and keep remembering all the great times we had together. I can't believe how much it hurts – I still keep bursting into tears. I don't think I'll ever be able to trust anyone again.

Freddie's feelings

I'm 15 and play street hockey with my local youth club. We've been doing really well and I made it on to the team that is touring some Dutch youth clubs this summer. It's a great team and I was really looking forward to the tour. Now it's all gone wrong! I broke my ankle at the weekend and I'm going to have to be replaced on the tour. I'm totally fed up. I know the team will have a brilliant time and I won't be part of it. By the time they get back, I won't really be part of their group any more. I'm feeling like an outsider already and I don't think I even want to go and see them off.

Activity 1

Read about how Anya and Freddie are feeling in Source 1. In pairs, choose one of them to respond to with some ideas that will help them to cope with their feelings of loss and move forward positively.

All loss can be painful to us but for many people the death of somebody they love is one of the most difficult things they may experience.

Source 2 Part of Prince William's speech to the Child Bereavement Charity of which he is the royal patron

… what I understand now, is that losing a close family member is one of the hardest experiences that anyone can ever endure.

Never being able to say the word 'mummy' again in your life sounds like a small thing. However, for many, including me, it is now really just a word – hollow and evoking only memories. I can therefore wholeheartedly relate to the Mother's Day Campaign as I too have felt – and still feel – the emptiness on such a day as Mother's Day.

Activity 2

Read Source 2 and discuss the following questions:
1 Is it helpful to hear famous people talk about their grief?
2 Does hearing famous people speak about grief make it OK for us to talk more openly?
3 If you were experiencing a strong sense of loss and grief what do you think would make it easier for you to cope?

Activity 3

Read Source 3 and discuss the following questions:
1 Do you think Sarah was too young to go her grandfather's funeral?
2 What are the arguments for and against letting children attend funerals?
3 Who should make the final decision about going to a funeral – the child or their parents/carers?

Activity 4

'Grief shouldn't be swept under the carpet …
grief needs to be brought out into the open, doesn't it?'
– spoken by a teenager whose dad had died.

What do you think could be done in school to help someone who is grieving?

Source 3 Going to funerals

My grandfather died when I was eleven. He lived with us for the last two years of his life and I was very close to him. My parents decided they wouldn't let me go to the funeral; they thought I was too young.

Sarah

I was nine when Auntie Liz died. I'm proud that I went to the funeral service and crematorium.

James

6.1 What do we need to keep healthy?

In this lesson you will learn:
- what 'being healthy' can mean
- the importance of healthy routines in life.

Starter

What does 'being healthy' mean? If you were going to find out if someone was a healthy person, what kind of questions would you ask them?

Activity 1

Design a questionnaire that helps you to find out if Year 7s in your school lead a healthy lifestyle. Start by working with another person to come up with five questions that would help you to decide. Don't just think about exercise and 'junk' food. What else affects a person's health?

Ten Ways to Stop Spreading Infections

✓ 1. Wash hands before touching food

✓ 2. Use a handkerchief/tissue when coughing or sneezing

✓ 3. Make sure used tissues go in the waste bin

✓ 4. Don't share combs or hairbrushes

✓ 5. Cover cuts with a dressing/plaster

✓ 6. Have vaccinations

✓ 7. Shower or bath regularly

✓ 8. Don't pick scabs or spots

✓ 9. Wash hands after going to the lavatory

✓ 10. Never spit

Source 1

Activity 2

If we build healthy routines into our lives we can help to keep ourselves and others healthy. Look at the list in Source 1 of what you can do to stop infections spreading. Work with a partner to come up with an example of an infection or disease that might be prevented if you took each action suggested.

Activity 3

Is your school a 'healthy school'? Imagine you are giving out awards for this. Work in groups to think about how you would rate these areas in your school, and give reasons for why you chose these ratings. As judges you are looking at the following areas:

- food
- playgrounds
- getting around the school
- lessons

- behaviour
- help and support
- pupils' views.

Rate each one of these as in the example below.

	Excellent	Good	Not bad	Poor	Awful
Food		✔ *We like the choices – it's good that healthy options are available*			

Public health campaigns in the media talk about the problems of obesity. There are clear dangers in being overweight. Unfortunately the media usually focuses on faddy diets to lose weight rather than healthy eating.

Diets based on only one or two foods may be successful in the short term, but can be dull and hard to stick to. The healthier, long-term way to lose weight is by eating a healthy, balanced diet and combining it with more physical activity.

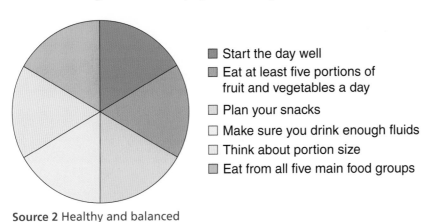

■ Start the day well
■ Eat at least five portions of fruit and vegetables a day
□ Plan your snacks
□ Make sure you drink enough fluids
□ Think about portion size
■ Eat from all five main food groups

Source 2 Healthy and balanced

Activity 4

People often have trouble with dieting because they try to do too much too soon. Look at Source 2. What's one first step a person could take for each of the six segments?

Activity 5

Go round the class completing this sentence: 'Healthy people are those who …'

In this lesson you will learn:
- that an appropriate balance between work, leisure and exercise can promote health
- to assess your own health profile.

Starter

Think back over the last 24 hours. Name one healthy thing you ate or drank, and one healthy activity you did. In a small group tell each other what you chose, and find out if others think you are healthy too.

Source 1 Being healthy means …

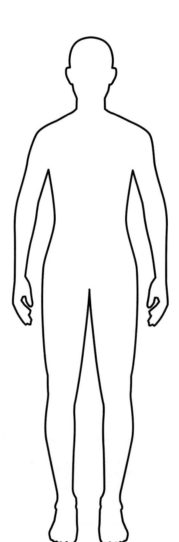

Eating healthily.

Balancing leisure, physical activity and rest.

Making sensible decisions about alcohol, cigarettes and other drugs.

Valuing and respecting yourself and others.

Caring for the environment.

Building good relationships with family and friends.

Keeping safe.

Dealing with stress or worry.

Enjoying growing up.

Activity 1

Look at the drawing and read the labels in Source 1. Think back to your questionnaires about health from the last lesson. Is anything missing from the picture?

1 First, it's time to reward yourself for what you are already doing well. Choose three areas from the picture where you are already doing something healthy, for example 'I make sure I get eight hours sleep every night'.

2 Now choose three areas where you think you need to make improvements to your lifestyle to become healthier. For example: do you eat five portions of fruit and vegetables each day? If not, set that as a challenge.

None of my friends does it.

I'd rather be online on the computer, watching TV or talking to friends.

Activity 2

What about exercise? Look at Source 2. These are typical excuses that a person might use to explain away why they don't take more exercise.

Come up with a quick one-sentence response to each that might get them to think again.

It's not cool.

Source 2 Three excuses

Source 3 Smile of the year

chatter

Come up with seven great tweets that would help them win #SmileChallenge

 Joe Bloggs @JoeBloggs

| Home | Find | Profile | Settings | Log out |

Activity 3

How important are teeth to good health? Look at Source 3. Imagine there's an award for 'Smile of the Year'. Your task is to write a daily tweet for a week reminding entrants of what to do to keep their mouth healthy.

Activity 4

What is one new thing you would do to up your personal health profile?

6.3 How do I keep healthy?

In this lesson you will learn:
- how to make decisions that affect your health
- about choices you can make to keep healthy.

Starter

Your life involves making choices. Think back over the day so far, from the time you woke up until now. What choices have you made today that could affect your health? These could be choices about washing, food, exercise and so on.

Activity 1

Look at Source 1 and make a meal plan for your family for a week.

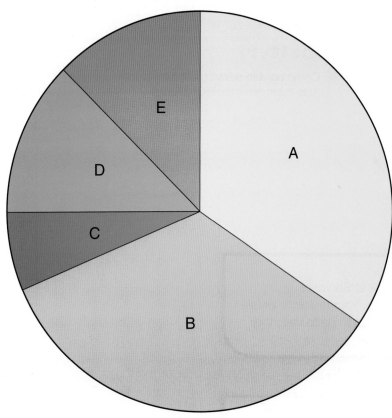

A Bread, other cereals and potatoes: these should be the basis of most of our meals; they give us energy.

B Fruit and vegetables: these contain many of the vitamins and minerals we need for good health; they help us to fight infections, which is very important to healthy eating.

C Foods containing fats and sugars: butter, eggs, cream, oil, biscuits, cakes, ice cream and so on; these should be eaten sparingly.

D Milk and dairy foods: milk, cheese, yoghurt; these keep bones and teeth strong and healthy so you should eat moderate amounts.

E Meats, fish, pulses and beans: good sources of protein, so eat moderate amounts.

Source 1 The five main food groups

The food traffic light system

If we want to healthily, one of the key things we should be doing is trying to cut down on fat (especially saturated fat), salt and added sugars.

With traffic light colours, you can see at a glance if the food you're looking at has high, medium or low amounts of fat, saturated fat, sugars and salt in 100g of the food (see Source 2).

Red = High   Amber = **Medium**   Green = **Low**

So, if you see a red light on the front of the pack, you know the food is high in something we should be trying to cut down on. It's fine to have the food occasionally, or as a treat, but try to keep an eye on how often you choose these foods, or try eating them in smaller amounts.

If you see amber, you know the food isn't high or low in the nutrient, so this is an OK choice most of the time, but you might want to go for green for that nutrient some of the time.

Green means the food is low in that nutrient. The more green lights, the healthier the choice.

	Fat			
LOW	7.7 g per serving			

	Saturates			
LOW	2.0 g per serving			

	Sugars			
HIGH	42.2 g per serving			

	Salt			
MED	2.0 g per serving			

SERVES 2 - HALF PACK PROVIDES

CALS	SUGAR	FAT	SAT FAT	SALT
350	2.0g	22.0g	9.8g	4.15g
18%	2%	31%	49%	69%

OF YOUR GUIDELINE DAILY AMOUNT

Source 2 Food traffic light system

Activity 2

Look again at Source 2. Use the system of traffic light colours displayed on foods, and suggest how you'd plan the family shopping, based on your meal plans from Activity 1.

Activity 3

Let's look at additives in foods. Some food additives used in hundreds of foods and drinks can cause behaviour changes and health issues. Read the information in Source 3 and decide which E-numbers you'd avoid if shopping for food for children.

If you look on food labels you will often see an 'E' with a number next to it. Most of the processed food we eat would not exist without these additives. You can tell what kind of additive it is by looking at the 'E' number.

E100 to E180	Colouring to make colourless food look more appetising
E200 to E297	Preservatives that artificially make food stay fresh by slowing down the growth of bacteria
E322 to E495	Emulsifiers and stabilisers keep different parts of a food together, for example air and liquid in ice cream
E620 to E640	Flavourings; some are natural, but artificial ones have E-numbers: they add flavour to food
E950 to E967	Sweeteners are used instead of sugar for artificial sweetness

Source 3 Food additives

Keeping healthy

All teenagers are different. Many like to spend their free time doing things like shopping, being with friends, gaming and other online activities such as social networking; others are into reading, watching films and playing sports.

A lot of the above will be done with friends – but it's also important for young people to continue having good relationships with their family. When asked, parents said they thought a good way of spending time with their teenagers could be going to see a film together, or even a quick meal or a drink in a café.

Seeing a film you're both interested in
Listening to music together at home or going to a concert
Going to a football game or other sports match
Checking out local events such as markets, festivals or environmental activities
Going away for a weekend to an event, such as a show or an exhibition
Cooking together
Going out for a meal together

Source 4 Parents' ideas for family time

Teenagers are spending an increasing amount of time in extracurricular activities such as dance classes, drama clubs and sports. They're also working hard at homework and often other extra studies. All this is important, but so is getting enough rest to do it all.

Most teenagers need eight to nine hours of sleep each night. Getting the right amount of sleep is essential for anyone who wants to do well on a test or play sports without stumbling. Unfortunately, though, many teenagers don't get enough sleep.

Experts say that during the teenage years, the body's sleep rhythms are temporarily reset, telling teenagers to fall asleep later and wake up later. This change might be due to the fact that the brain hormone melatonin is produced later at night for teenagers than it is for children and adults.

Are you getting enough sleep?

By the time you have become a teenager the NHS will have asked you and your family to think about a range of immunisations. The national immunisation programme has meant that dangerous diseases such as tetanus, diphtheria and polio have practically disappeared in the UK. But these diseases could come back – they still exist in Europe and throughout the world. That's why it's so important for you to protect yourself.

How does immunisation work?

Vaccines work by stimulating the body's immune system to make antibodies (substances to fight infections and diseases). So if you come into contact with the infection, the antibodies will recognise it and protect you.

Source 5 Typical UK immunisation programme

Age	Vaccine
2 months	5-in-1 vaccine – this single jab protects against: diphtheria, tetanus, pertussis (whooping cough), polio and Hib type B (a bacterial infection that can cause severe pneumonia or meningitis in young children) Pneumonia vaccine Rotavirus vaccine
3 months	5-in-1 vaccine, second dose Meningitis C Rotavirus vaccine, second dose
4 months	5-in-1 vaccine, third dose Pneumonia vaccine, second dose
Between 12 and 13 months	Hib/Meningitis C booster, given as a single jab Measles, mumps and rubella (MMR) vaccine Pneumonia vaccine, third dose
2 to 3 years	Flu vaccine (annual)
3 years and 4 months, or soon after	Measles, mumps and rubella (MMR) vaccine, second dose 4-in-1 pre-school booster: single jab containing vaccines against diphtheria, tetanus, whooping cough (pertussis) and polio
Around 12 to 13 years	HPV vaccine
Around 13 to 15 years	Meningitis C booster
Around 13 to 18 years	3-in-1 teenage booster: single jab vaccines against diphtheria, tetanus and polio
Age 65 and over	Flu (every year) Pneumonia vaccine

Activity 6

Look at Source 5. Some of you will have had or are soon going to have the HPV vaccine (see 12–13 years). Use a website like www.nhs.uk or another source to find the answers to the following questions:
1 What is HPV?
2 Who is entitled to the HPV vaccine in the UK?
3 What does the vaccine do?

Activity 7

What is the one thing you would remove from the world that would instantly make it a healthier place? Why?

In this lesson you will:
- identify some rights and ages of responsibility
- think about the importance of 'confidentiality'
- find out about your rights to health and treatment.

Source 1 Rights for young people. Taken from a summary guide written by the Childrens Rights Alliance for England: www.crae.org.uk/rights/uncrc.html

The UK government has agreed to uphold a set of international human rights for young people that mean:

You should be treated with respect at all times

You should be consulted whenever decisions are made about you

You should never be treated unfairly because of your ethnic origin, sex, any disabilities, your religion or beliefs, your sexual orientation or your transgender status.

Starter

Look at Source 1. As you get older you gain other rights and become legally able to do a variety of things. At what age do you think you can:

a open a bank account in your own name
b get a part-time job – with some restrictions
c have a tattoo
d ride a moped of up to 50cc?

As a young person gains different rights they may realise that some of these rights involve sharing personal or sensitive information. We often want this information to be kept confidential.

Age 11

Being able to talk to someone in private.

Not gossiping.

Source 2 Confidentiality – what is it?

Age 12–13

When someone will not tell people about what you have said until you want them to.

Age 15–16

Very important … The information given by anyone should be kept in absolute trust.

When my information should only be shared with my permission.

Having the option to keep something private.

Activity 1

Read what the young people in Source 2 have said about confidentiality. In pairs:
1 Discuss which of these definitions is the best.
2 Come up with your own definition of the word 'confidentiality'.

One of the situations where we want confidential care is when we see someone about personal health problems. Young people under sixteen are entitled to have their confidential information treated in exactly the same way as adults. Your health care will more often than not be something you happily discuss with your parents. However, sometimes you may wish to discuss things in private.

a) At what age can I see a doctor on my own?

c) Can I be sure that I'll be treated in confidence by a nurse or doctor?

b) Can I choose my own doctor?

Source 3 Seeing someone about your health

Picture posed by models

d) Can I get confidential advice about anything to do with sex if I'm under sixteen?

Activity 2

Look at Source 3. The photographs show young people using health services. The questions in the speech bubbles are often asked by young people who are unsure of their rights. In groups, consider these worries. What would you say to reassure each questioner?
You could use the Brook website, www.brook.org.uk, to help you answer some of these questions.

Activity 3

Complete this sentence: 'One useful piece of information I have gained from this lesson is …'

7.1 What do we mean by 'risk'?

In this lesson you will learn about:
- what 'risk' can mean
- positive and negative risks
- different attitudes to risk.

> Trying is the first step towards failure.

As said by Homer Simpson
Source 1 Do you believe Homer is right?

Starter

Look at Source 1. In your group, discuss whether Homer is right.

Everything you do in life has the possibility of a good or bad outcome – you can think of these as positive or negative risks.

A positive risk is one where you are doing something because you hope that you will gain something, improve yourself or enjoy yourself. An example might be speaking in front of the class – this may improve your communication skills and build your confidence.

A negative risk is one with an outcome that could harm you or someone else. An example might be consuming alcohol before riding a bike or driving a car – this can endanger you and others.

Activity 1

Look at Source 2. Do these photos suggest anything about 'risk' to you? If so, what? Share your ideas with someone else.

Source 2 Risky, or not?

Crossing a busy road

Playing the lottery

Speaking in assembly

Activity 2

In pairs, look at Source 3 and make a note of how probable you think each event is. Then decide:
- which of these things are completely down to chance
- which we could have some control over
- how we could reduce the risk involved where we have some control.

Smoking cigarettes

Source 3 What are the chances …?

	Never going to happen	Probably won't happen	50 / 50	It could happen	Definitely will happen
Being caught playing truant					
Getting heads when you flip a coin					
Getting drunk after drinking alcohol					
Winning the jackpot on a lottery					
Cycling your way to the moon					
Going to prison for carrying a knife					
You winning a national TV talent show					
Tall parents having a tall child					
Getting heads each time you flip a coin, six times in a row					
The sun rising tomorrow morning					

When we think about reducing risks, we are probably thinking about the harm that taking that risk might cause. So we need to think about two things:
- the *what* – the harm that might happen to us
- the *might* – the likelihood that harm will happen to us.

Take the example of an aeroplane crash. The chance of being harmed if an aeroplane crashes is high. However, the likelihood of this happening is low, because so few planes crash compared with the large numbers that fly every day.

So, would you be happy to fly in an aeroplane?

Activity 3

Can you think of any other examples that show the difference between the 'what' and the 'might'? Here's an idea to get you started:

Activity	What …	Might …
Bungee jumping	Bungee snaps	Highly unlikely if equipment is regularly checked, assessed and the company is professionally validated

Activity 4

Before you started today's lesson you may only have thought of risk as a negative thing. What's the best positive risk you've ever taken?

7.2 How do we manage risky situations?

In this lesson you will:
- learn about how to respond in risky situations
- recognise some ways to keep yourself safe.

Starter

Think back to the previous lesson and remind yourself of the meaning of the word 'risk'. What definition would you give?

Activity 1

Where do you think you are most at risk?
Here are four locations where accidents might happen to someone your age:
- On the road or in car parks
- In or around the home
- In school
- On a sports field/in a sports hall (while doing sport)

Where do you think an accident is most likely to happen? Rank the locations in order of most dangerous to least dangerous.

It isn't always obvious when we might be at risk – we need to think and plan to keep safe. This will help us reduce the risk of something bad happening. Risk can never be completely ruled out – but there are ways in which we can think about a situation and reduce the risks.

Activity 2

Look at the situations in Source 2, and use the four steps in Source 1 to help you work out what you could do.

How to deal with a risky situation

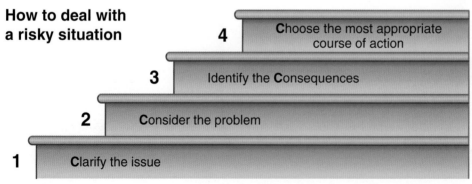

4 **C**hoose the most appropriate course of action

3 Identify the **C**onsequences

2 **C**onsider the problem

1 **C**larify the issue

Source 1

Source 2 Risky situations?

It's a sunny day in the summer holidays and you and your friends are spending the day in the park. Some of the group decide that climbing to the top of one of the trees would be a great idea.

You have spent the day at a friend's house. You have been told you have to be back home by 6pm. You thought you had allowed plenty of time but you've missed the bus and the battery has died on your mobile phone. It's getting late. You know you're going to be in trouble if you're not home on time.

You and your friends are at a party. Everyone is helping themselves to food and drink. People are behaving as if they are a bit drunk. You want to keep in with everyone in your group but you don't want to drink alcohol. One of your mates offers you a bottle of something alcoholic.

Activity 3

In Activity 2 you looked at how you could deal with risky situations that could arise. However, there are some sensible precautions we could all take to keep ourselves safe.
Look at the safety suggestions in Source 3. Put each of them under one of the following three headings:
● Travelling safely
● Feeling under threat
● Looking after personal possessions

Activity 4

Think about how you would complete this sentence:
'The most important safety message I've learnt from today's lesson is …
because ….'
Share your sentence with one other person.

Source 3 Safety suggestions. Information from the charity Kidscape and teenagers in conversation

Think twice about using the latest phone model, iPod, etc. in public places – expensive equipment could attract potential thieves and muggers.

If you are threatened, yell and run away, if possible.

If you are being followed, go into a shop or towards people or try crossing the road to see if the person follows.

Never hitchhike or take rides from strangers and try to avoid walking home alone.

Avoid taking short-cuts through dark or deserted places.

Don't walk around outside listening on headphones as this prevents you being aware of what is happening around you.

If someone approaches you asking directions and they make you feel uncomfortable, keep your distance or walk away.

Avoid empty carriages on trains.

7.3 How do I practise refusal skills?

In this lesson you will:
- consider how good communication can help us reduce risks
- learn about refusal skills
- practise refusal skills.

Source 1 Why is it hard to say 'no'?

Starter

Look at Source 1. Think about a time when you wanted to say 'no' to somebody but found that hard to do. For example, your friend asked you to go out that night but you actually just wanted to stay home with your family. Why was it hard to say 'no'?

Saying 'no' isn't always easy. This might be because we don't want to hurt someone's feelings, or we might feel left out or different from the group.

In the last activity you discussed how it can be difficult to say 'no' in a variety of situations and to various people. There are some clear ways of communicating with people that mean we don't have to end up doing something we don't want to do. These are:
- actively listening to the other person (see lesson 10.2)
- being assertive (see lesson 5.2)
- using refusal skills – we use these when we feel we might be harmed or in danger.

Activity 1

1 What things have you said 'no' to?
2 What have other people said 'no' to you about?
3 Is it important to be able to say 'no'?

Here are some simple techniques for saying 'no':

How to say 'no'

- Simply say 'no' or 'no thanks'.
- Be direct, for example 'No, I don't want to do that.'
- Be a broken record – repeat 'no' over and over again or use variations to make your point: 'No, I'm not interested', 'Not me!', 'No, never'.
- Walk away – if they won't accept your 'no' then it's time to go!

Source 1

Activity 2

Source 1 lists some simple techniques for saying 'no'.
Practise these skills by moving around your group – each time you meet a different person imagine you have to say 'no' in a new way.

Remember, it's not about the volume you use or an aggressive tone – saying 'no' in a calm, quiet way is often much more effective than raising your voice.

Activity 3

Imagine that one of your really good friends asks you to join in with something you don't want to do, saying 'I think you'll really enjoy this. Give it a try.'

Come up with five different sentences that you could use to refuse them. Make sure your responses are calm, assertive and polite.

Activity 4

Refusal skills are part of a range of ways that we can communicate to keep ourselves safe and to reduce risks. Give yourself a rating for how well you think you can use these three different communication skills:

	I can do this really well	I'm fairly good at this	I need to practise this more
Active listening			
Being assertive			
Saying 'no'			

7.4 How can we tackle bullying?

In this lesson you will learn:
- how to prevent bullying from happening
- the importance of speaking out against bullying.

Everyone – children, teachers, adults – can help put a stop to bullying.

There are lots of reasons why some people start bullying, and why others are bullied. There is something about all of us that others might pick on – but bullying, at school or outside school, is always wrong, no matter what.

Starter

There is never a justifiable reason for bullying. Ever. Bullying at school can happen for lots of reasons. Why do bullies single people out? What sort of things do they pick on?

Peter's story

We had this PE teacher and he thought anyone who wasn't good at games was stupid. I'm really small for my age and not much good at PE. He started picking on me in lessons. Then he started calling me a wimp and other things. It doesn't sound much. I mean, he never touched me or pushed me around or anything, so when I tried to tell my mum, it did sound rather pathetic.

Source 1

Rachel's story

Source 2

It all started when my mum got married again. I liked my new step-sister. She was older than me and I really looked up to her. When she moved in, though, her friends came round all the time and made life difficult for me. She kept putting me down with comments about how I looked. She said if I told Mum I'd be in trouble and I'd split the family up. Then she started threatening me and saying that if I didn't tidy her room she'd tell Mum I was rude to her. I did try talking to Mum but she was so happy I didn't want to spoil things for her.

Anne's story

I was new at the school – joining halfway through the year – and break times were the worst. This group of pupils used to hang around by these seats that were out of sight of the school windows and that's why they went there. At first, they were friendly and chatty and, being new, I was really pleased that they let me be part of their group. Then they wanted me to buy cigarettes for them. I said I didn't smoke and that's when it started. They got all the other pupils in the class to completely blank me, and started sending horrible texts to me. Then someone hacked into my online profile and made stuff up about me.

Source 3

Activity 1

Read Sources 1, 2 and 3 about young people's experiences of being bullied. Suggest three ways in which each young person could begin to tackle their situation.

Activity 2

How do you think your school creates a positive atmosphere in which pupils support and help each other? Are there additional things that you can suggest? In and around school, what could pupils in Year 7 do to prevent bullying happening in the first place?

Bystanders are people who do not act while someone else is being bullied. They are not the ringleaders but sometimes they may join in with name calling.

Activity 3

Have you ever seen bullying happening and not known what to do? Look at Source 4 – these are statements from young people who were bystanders. What would you say to each bystander to encourage them to help?

'I knew the photo was faked. It was horrible and stupid, but if I didn't take part in sending it round I knew they'd do the same to me.'

'He showed me the text message he'd got. It was really mean.'

'My friend went on and on about being bullied – I got tired of listening to her.'

'There weren't any adults around when it was happening.'

Source 4 Bystanders' words

'Sticks and stones may break my bones but words will never hurt me.'
(Often quoted but not at all true.)

'Why are they all so big, other children? So noisy?...
Lived all their lives in playgrounds.
Spent years inventing games that don't let me in.'
Roger McGough

'Give us another 10p or get another bash For being you.'
Mick Gowar

Source 5 The hurt and pain of bullying

Activity 4

Read the words in Source 5 that have been written about bullying. They all focus on the hurt and pain that bullying can cause. Compose a verse or piece of prose, of no more than five lines, that could inspire somebody to speak out against bullying or gain the courage to do something positive.

In this lesson you will:
- learn about 'risking on purpose'
- practise assessing and managing risk
- think about balancing health and safety with personal choices.

Starter

Think back over what you have learnt about risk in previous lessons. What does the expression 'taking a positive risk' mean?

THE EXPERIENCE CENTRE

We can offer you the time of your life and get your adrenalin buzzing! Try the most scary thrills – feel the fear and do it anyway!

White-water rafting   Zip-wire   Go-karting

Source 1 Taking risks on purpose

Activity 1

Imagine your year group is planning a day at the Experience Centre. Your teachers will have completed a thorough risk assessment – and they want you too to think about how to plan an event like this. Discuss the topic you have been given, weigh up the risks and then present your findings as a brilliant challenge rather than a potential nightmare.

Wanting to take risks on purpose is natural and is how we learn to progress in life. It helps us to understand our own boundaries and build our resilience. At every stage in our lives we take small (and sometimes big) steps to grow in our independence. Adults also try different things in order to gain new experiences and insights.

Activity 2

Some people laugh at health and safety rules (and, sometimes, they can be taken to extremes) but they are an important part of managing risk. It's obvious why health and safety rules (which are a type of risk assessment) are important at an activity centre.

Discuss how young people can use risk assessment skills to keep themselves safe in other situations.

Different people have very different attitudes to risk-taking, even when what they are doing is within safety guidelines and is regulated. At an activity centre people will want to try different things, some appearing more risky than others. Some people enjoy taking personal risks by doing extreme sports or going on wild adventure holidays.

The idea is to test body and mind against personal limits.

You have to have the guts to call it a day when it gets too tough.

Society needs to accept that accidents happen without it always being someone's fault.

It's not just a physical challenge, it's a mental challenge too. Your lungs are bursting, your muscles are burning but you just don't give in.

When I finish the event I'm glowing with pride because I've tested myself and succeeded.

Source 2 Extreme sport – what do you think?

Activity 3

Look at Source 2 – it shows of a photo of parkour – a sport which involves trying to get around or through obstacles in the quickest way possible. Parkour can include running, climbing, swinging, vaulting, jumping, rolling and so on.

Discuss these questions:
- Why do some people feel the need to take part in sports like parkour?
- Do you think people should be allowed to take part in very risky sports like parkour?
- Why do some people think such sports should be banned?

Activity 4

What is the biggest risk (physical or otherwise) that you have taken (when you risked something on purpose)? What did you gain from doing it?

7.6 Can gambling be good?

In this lesson you will:
- discuss your understanding of what 'gambling' means
- consider the risks attached to gambling
- explore attitudes to gambling and gamblers.

Source 1 Gambling, the law and you: The Gambling Act 2005

- National Lottery – you can buy, play and sell National Lottery tickets and scratch cards from the age of sixteen.
- Football pools – you can bet on the pools from the age of sixteen.
- Bingo – you allowed into a bingo club at any age but have to be eighteen or over to participate.
- Betting shop – no one under eighteen is allowed on the premises or to place a bet.
- Casinos – you are not allowed into a casino under the age of eighteen.
- Gaming machines – children under eighteen can only play low-stake, low pay-out machines – often found in seaside arcades or theme parks.
- Online/mobile gambling via the internet or an app – also comes under the legislation restricting this to adults: you are not allowed to play if you are under eighteen.

> One way to define gambling is: it usually involves two or more people risking a stake (usually money or other valuables) on an uncertain outcome, which is partly determined by chance. The stake is paid by the loser to the winner.
> *Paul Bellringer, Director of Responsible Gambling Solutions*

Source 2 Young people and gambling

- 85% of young people aged between eleven and fifteen did not gamble in 2012.
- 95% of young people aged between eleven and fifteen did not buy National Lottery tickets or scratch cards.
- 80% of young people aged between eleven and fifteen who looked at the National Lottery website did this on behalf of their parents.
- Girls are more likely than boys to check their parents' numbers and watch the National Lottery TV shows with their parents.
- Boys are more likely than girls to gamble in general.
- Young people from less wealthy families are more likely to gamble their own money.
- Gambling is a habit-forming activity: if you have practised gambling games for free, you are more likely to gamble money on other games.

Starter

What does 'gambling' mean? Draw a mind map and write down any words that you think of when you hear the word 'gambling'.

Activity 1

Look at Source 2 which tells you a few facts about gambling and young people your age.
- Why do some people choose to gamble?
- Why do some people choose not to gamble?

Source 3 Pop-up gambling?

Scratchcards

Activity 2

Look at Source 3. What is happening in the cartoon?
What amazing things do pop-up adverts offer people on the internet?
Why do gambling websites use pop-ups?

Playing cards

Activity 3

People have very different attitudes to gambling. Use the worksheet your teacher will give you to find out some of the attitudes in your class.

Activity 4

How have your attitudes towards gambling changed as a result of this lesson?

Casino chips to exchange for money

7.7 How do I reduce risks?

In this lesson you will learn:
- how to minimise harm and keep safe in various situations
- about basic first aid: the recovery position
- to think about your own personal safety
- how to apply personal safety rules when using the internet.

Starter

Here are three examples of when health and safety must be considered – for your protection and everyone else's:
- A group of your friends have a day out cycling.
- Your youth group spends the day travelling the canal on a barge.
- You are signing up for a new app.

Come up with at least three safety rules to follow for one of these situations.

Activity 1

In pairs, practise putting each other into the recovery position.

Health and safety rules apply in everyday life. There are always things you can do to help others when they're hurt. As you get older you'll become more aware of how to help yourself and others. You may already have learnt about making an emergency call by dialling 999. Here's some more potentially life-saving information:

- If someone collapses and you know that they've taken pills or alcohol, tell the ambulance crew when they arrive.
- While someone else is calling for help, you could try to put the person into the recovery position (see Source 1).

Activity 2

Look at www.juniorcitizen.org. uk. If you could add one more topic icon to this page, what would it be and why?

Source 1 The recovery position

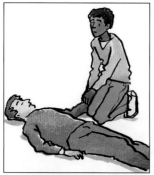 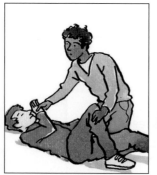 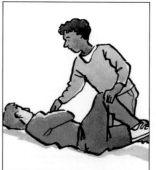 

1 Place the arm nearest you at a right angle to the person's body.

2 Bring the far arm across the person's chest and place the back of their hand against their cheek. Bend the person's far leg at the knee.

3 While keeping the person's hand pressed against their cheek, pull the knee towards you, rolling the person towards you and onto their side.

4 Stay with the person until help arrives.

Health and safety rules also apply when using the internet. For example, people need to be sensible when buying things online. You should only shop on a reliable website, make sure you only give payment information on a secure site and so on. You also need to know how to be safe with your personal information.

Social networking has become a part of everyday life for many people across the globe. You can talk to anyone, anywhere, anytime online. This is an amazing use of technology. However, just like anything else, fantastic inventions can also end up being misused.

Research says that more than a quarter of eight- to eleven-year-olds claimed to have a profile page on a social networking website. This is despite age restrictions aimed at preventing pre-teens from using such sites.

Activity 3

Look at Source 2. You are at, or approaching, the age when you may choose to sign up to a social networking site.

In preparation for that, here are some recommendations that are worth considering. Explain why it is important to follow these guidelines.

1 Be as anonymous as possible.
2 Protect your information.
3 Be honest about your age.
4 Think before posting any photos.
5 Avoid meeting in person.
6 Check your profile or page regularly for comments.

Source 2 Social networking

Activity 4

Go to www.saferinternet.org.uk/safer-internet-day/2013/quiz and try out the quiz that is all about using the internet safely.

Activity 5

More information about safety online can be found at www.saferinternet.org.uk. Go to the 'Advice and resources' section and choose your age group.

How do the suggestions in this section help somebody deal with bullying online?

7.8 Who can help me keep safe?

In this lesson you will:
- explore a range of issues which affect personal safety
- use a 'community of enquiry' model to explore these issues
- identify agencies that can help with these problems.

This lesson covers several issues which may affect the personal safety of people your age. You may already know about these issues or you may not have thought about them. They can affect people in all kinds of communities and situations – not just in large cities, or in groups that the media choose to highlight. Wherever we live and whoever we are, we need to be aware of these issues and how we might be able to help.

> Just to know that your son or daughter went out to have a good time … and then they don't come home. You don't think that's ever going to happen.

> Saying you carried it for defence can't be an excuse.

> I had some many high hopes for him. I never thought he would carry a knife.

> Friends and family are always left to pick up the pieces.

Source 1 Knife crime

Starter

Look at Source 1.
Apart from the victim and the offender, think about who else is affected by the issue:
a) locally
b) nationally
c) globally.

Source 2 Gang culture

Headline News

You can be ex-gang but you can never be an ex-murderer

Nicola Dyer shakes with bitter anger as she describes the fatal stabbing of her 16-year-old son Shakilus Townsend in a trap staged by London gang members four years ago

The youngsters, identified by police as being linked to street crime, stop slouching in front of Nicola. They are attentive. The mum of five tells them:

'Five years ago my son was killed. He was chased down in the street like he was an animal, and then stabbed and beaten to death.

'Young people talk about joining a gang as being like a family, but I would like to

know what sort of family you get from that? What kind of family would beat and stab somebody?

'You have one chance to make something of your lives.

'You can be ex-gang members, but you can't be ex-murderers.'

Discuss 1

How do you feel after reading this story?

Source 3 Child sexual exploitation
Adapted extracts from the Local Government Association booklet: *CSE Myth vs Reality*

Discuss 2

Did anything surprise you in Source 3?

Five myths about Child Sexual Exploitation (CSE)

Myth #1: CSE usually follows a particular pattern of events
Reality: It can take many different forms and can be carried out by individuals (lone perpetrators), by street gangs or by groups. It can be motivated by money, i.e. child prostitution, or personal sexual gratification.

Myth #2: It only happens in certain ethnic/cultural communities
Reality: Both perpetrators and victims come from a variety of ethnic and cultural backgrounds. CSE is not restricted to the groups highlighted by the media.

Myth #3: It only happens to children in care
Reality: The majority of CSE victims live at home. However, looked-after children account for a disproportionate number of victims and can be particularly vulnerable.

Myth #4: It only happens to girls and young women by adult men
Reality: Boys and young men are also targeted. Peer-on-peer child sexual exploitation happens too. Young people are sometimes used to 'recruit' others. Young men are less likely to tell anyone or seek support, often due to stigma, prejudice or embarrassment or the fear that no one will believe them.

Myth #5: This only happens in large towns and cities
Reality: Evidence shows that CSE is not restricted to urban areas such as large towns and cities but also happens in rural areas such as villages and coastal areas.

Go to www.thehideout.org.uk, click on the 'Young people's page', then 'Teenspeak' in the lefthand bar and watch the video.

Source 4 Domestic violence: screenshot of homepage offering help

Discuss 3

What do you think the button 'cover your tracks' is for?

Discuss 4

How do you feel after reading these stories?

Michael lives in Hertfordshire.

I came out to friends in school about a year and a half ago. It was between me and a few good friends but of course the whole school knew within a couple of days. The hassle I received was intolerable, to say the least. When I finally plucked up the courage to speak to a teacher, very little was done.

Although my head of year was understanding, she acted as if it were a normal everyday case of 'teasing in the playground'. I gave her a list of names of people I knew to be causing a problem but when she spoke to them it got worse.

Michael

Holly lives in Hampshire.

I decided to come out when I was in Year 8 at school. It took me about three months to build up the courage to tell anyone as I had heard of people being bullied, assaulted and even killed because of their sexuality but I felt I had to in order to live a normal life.

Holly

I came out to my best friend first and she said she had already thought so anyway and she didn't mind. So I felt great and I thought that everyone else would be fine about it.

But I couldn't have been more wrong. People close to me were fine as they, knowing me better than others, had already guessed but other people in my school who found out were nasty, calling me all the names they could think of and they could be threatening, saying things like they were going to beat me up because they thought I was disgusting.

Source 5 Homophobia: two stories

Female Genital Mutilation (FGM) is a harmful traditional practice that involves the partial or total removal of the female genitalia.
According to the most recent estimates, 66,000 women and girls have undergone FGM in England and Wales, while 24,000 girls under the age of eleven are at risk of undergoing it. However, despite the fact that FGM has been illegal in the UK since 1985, there has never been a single prosecution.

Discuss 5

Are you surprised or shocked by anything in Source 6?

Source 6 Female genital mutilation
Source: 'A Statistical Study to Estimate the Prevalence of Female Genital Mutilation in England and Wales' published by FORWARD, October 2007

A forced marriage is where one or both people do not consent to the marriage, and pressure or abuse is used to keep them in it.

The pressure put on people to marry against their will can be physical (including threats, actual physical violence and sexual violence) or emotional and psychological (for example, when someone is made to feel like they're bringing shame on their family). Financial abuse (taking a person's wages or not giving them any money) can also be a factor.

Discuss 6

What else do you know or have you heard about forced marriage?

Source 7 Forced marriage
Case study text from www.forcedmarriage.net

Lena's story

My father found out that I had a boyfriend and that changed everything in our family. He literally kept me prisoner in the house, wouldn't let me see my friends and then started planning my wedding – to a man I had never met! He said that I had to follow our customs, and there would be no discussion. I had no way out …

Lena

Raj's story

People don't realise that men can also find themselves in this situation. I don't know if I could have told anyone even if I'd had the chance to. It's not exactly macho, is it, admitting that you were held hostage by your family and forced to marry someone you'd never even met?

Raj

Search for these organisations when seeking help or advice – for yourself or other people:

Knife crime . . . . www.droptheweapons.org/

Gang culture . . . . http://safe.met.police.uk/gangs_and_violence/pressure_from_your_mates.html

Child Sexual Exploitation . . . . www.thinkuknow.co.uk/ Teachers/Exploited/

Domestic violence . . . . http://safe.met.police.uk/domestic_violence_and_abuse/concerned_a_mate_worried_theyre_a_victim.html

Homophobia . . . . www.bbc.co.uk/radio1/advice/ factfile_az/homophobia

Female Genital Mutilation . . . . www.nspcc.org.uk/news-and-views/our-news/child-protectionnews/female-genital-mutilation-helpline/fgm-helpline-launched_wda96863.html

Forced marriage . . . . www.gov.uk/stop-forced-marriage

Source 8 Helping agencies

7.9 Where can I find help on …?

In this lesson you will:
- consider the warning signals that tell us when we need help
- identify some sources of help and support that people your age might need
- learn about different ways of responding to problem situations
- design information for people in school like yourselves to use.

Starter

'The best way to escape from a problem is to solve it.'
- What does this quotation mean?
- Can you think of examples of people you know who have overcome their problems by facing up to them?
- Is it always easy to find a solution?

Activity 1

Work with another person to list some other warning signals that people might experience.

Facing up to problems isn't easy. Some problems worry or frighten us so much that our bodies react to them physically. Think of the different ways people describe this:

Source 1 Warning signals

'I had a sinking feeling.'

'I could feel butterflies in my stomach.'

'I broke out in a cold sweat.'

Activity 2

Where would you advise someone experiencing their warning signals to look for information, help or support? Work in pairs to identify where you could go for help:
- in school
- in the local area
- using helplines or other media.

Remember to identify individuals who could help as well as organisations that might be useful.

Source 1 shows warning signals made by your body to tell you that you:
- feel at risk
- are worried that you are have a huge problem
- may be facing a new challenge.

We may experience warning signals when we feel unsafe or when we are about to do something unfamiliar or new, for example, when we have to stand up and present a report in class, audition for a play or try out for a sports team. They even happen when we know that at the other end of the experience we may get something good, such as a good grade, a good part or a place on the team.

Always pay attention to your warning signals and ask yourself:
- Do I really want to do this thing/take this step?
- What could be the result of doing it?
- Who could I ask for help and support when I do it?

Source 2 The Helping Hand

Activity 3

Look at Source 2. It suggests five things to do that can help us face up to our problems.

Work in a small group to discuss the five suggestions. Decide which of them might help someone in each of the following situations and explain how they would go about following the advice:
- Getting behind with homework or project work
- Losing or damaging something you borrowed from a friend
- Feeling bullied by other pupils

Activity 4

Think about suggestion 3 (the middle finger) on The Helping Hand.
- Who would be your trusted person(s) to turn to for advice?
- Why do you trust them?

Young people often have lots of questions that they would like help with. These questions may be about subjects such as drugs, emotions, HIV, relationships and money. They may also want information about exam worries or friendship problems.

So far this lesson has thought about people you can turn to for help and support. Many young people know that the internet can also be a good source of advice and information.

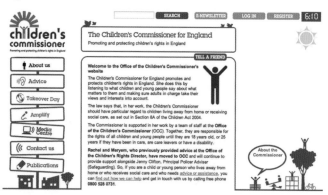

Source 3 www.childrenscommissioner.gov.uk
The Commissioner and her team make sure that adults in charge listen to children and young people.

The role of the Children's Commissioner for England was created by the Children Act 2004 and amended by the Children and Families Act 2014. The Commissioner promotes and protects children's rights. She is responsible for the rights of all children and young people in England with a particular focus on those who live away from home or who are in receipt of social care.

Source 4 www.childline.org.uk/Pages/Home.aspx
This is a national charity website that covers all sorts of issues that may affect young people.

Many websites, such as those in Sources 3 and 4, provide information and support to young people.

Some websites are easier to use than others and the quality of information varies from site to site. The next activity asks you to investigate some specific and popular sites.

Activity 5

Working in groups, your task is to look at a source of information for young people. You may be asked to look at one of the websites in Sources 3 or 4 or another one that your teacher will give you.

Your task is to investigate it, sample how it works and produce a review to help others decide if it is a useful source of advice and help. You will share your review with the rest of the class.

1   Your group should consider the following:
    ● Was it easy to read?
    ● Was it easy to navigate your way around the website and find more information?
    ● Was it interesting to look at?
    ● Would you recommend it as a source of help?
    Give examples to explain your responses.

2   Once your group has answered these questions, sum up your review of the website by giving it a score out of 10.
    As a general guide:
    ● 3/10   Not very useful, hard to find information and so on
    ● 5/10   Average usefulness – worth a look
    ● 7/10   Has got some useful things in it but could be improved (say how)
    ● 10/10   Great advice, well presented

Activity 6

Design a poster or webpage that highlights some of the sources of information that got high marks in your class. On your poster it should be clear:
● what these sources of information are
● why they are useful
● where people can find them.

Your school may already have a 'help and information for pupils' noticeboard or section of its website. You could ask for your poster or webpage to be displayed there. Remember that you will need to check with the pupils or staff who organise this noticeboard or part of the website to see if there are special requirements for displaying the information.

If your school doesn't have anything like this, then your year group could take on the task of asking your School Council (or other pupil organisation) to set one up.

Activity 7

Think back over the large amount of information in this lesson. Can you identify a new fact or a helping person/agency you hadn't heard of until today?

8.1 Who am I?

Starter

'All I'd really like out of life is to be normal.'
What do you think the young person who said this meant?

What is 'normal'?

Activity 1

Imagine you are asked to choose three items, small enough to fit into a bag to bring to school, to represent important aspects of your life. What would you include in your 'bits of me' bag? You now have one minute to share information about what those items are and what they represent for you. When everyone in your group has listened to each other, make a quick note of how you felt having everyone listen to you for a full minute.

:) It's easy to share how I feel when …

:| It's hard to share how I feel when …

:) I feel best when …

:(I feel uncomfortable around people when …

:| I am most comfortable in my class/form when …

:(At school I'm most concerned when …

:) I'm at my happiest when …

Source 1 Me and my feelings

Activity 2

Read the stems in Source 1 and complete the sentences.

Activity 3

> Great things are achieved not by impulse, but by a series of small things brought together.

Vincent van Gogh (1853–90), artist of 'Sunflowers' and 'Starry Night'

We all have different abilities, talents and ambitions, and yet we are often encouraged to be modest and not 'show off' about what we do well. But today is different: you now have the chance to talk with one other person about yourself.

You must mention what you are talented at, what your best skills are, what personal qualities you have that make you special, and what things you have accomplished, or perhaps even received awards for. See the example in Source 2.

'I am talented at illustrating my work with neat drawings. I'm skilled at map reading and never get lost if I've had time to plan a route. One of the personal qualities that makes me special is that I'm friendly and other people feel comfortable talking with me. I have an amazing imagination that takes me to the places I dream about.'

Source 2 My personal qualities

Activity 4

Think about how you would complete this sentence:
'The most important positive thing I've learnt about myself from today's lesson is … because …'
Share your sentence with one other person.

8.2 What does 'family' mean?

In this lesson you will learn:
- about different types of families
- that our family relationships affect our wellbeing.

Source 1 Different types of family

Starter

Look at the photos in Source 1 and see if you can come up with some answers to these questions:

- What do you think these families might have in common with each other?
- Does a family always live together? Why might they live in different houses or places?
- What makes a group of people a family?
- Family members don't always get on with each other. What sort of things can go wrong on a day-to-day basis? For example, a brother and sister falling out over whose turn it is to wash up the dishes.

Activity 1

Family arguments are easily started, but not so easy to stop. Read Source 2 and then discuss these questions:

1 How do you think Harry and Tom felt when they heard their parents arguing?
2 How far was Tom to blame for this argument starting?
3 How far was Harry to blame for this argument starting?
4 What could each family member do to calm the situation?
5 What could each family member do to avoid repeating it?

David and Sheila have been married for fourteen years. They have two children, Tom aged twelve and Harry who is nine. David's job has got more difficult recently, and he is staying longer in the office. Sheila has returned to work, to bring extra money into the home. But both parents can find themselves tired and irritable when they get home from work.

One summer evening Tom couldn't be bothered to do the washing up, even though it was his turn. Instead, he went out on his bike with some mates.

Harry hadn't done his homework and was moaning about it. Sheila and David got into an argument about who had given Tom permission to go out, and why Harry hadn't finished his homework.

David started having a go at Sheila for being too tired after the day at work to discipline the children. A really loud shouting match started between them. Harry and Tom overheard Sheila saying, 'It's not just down to me to get the boys to behave. You're their father. It's as if you're married to the office...'.

Source 2 David, Sheila, Tom and Harry

Source 3 Talking about families

Activity 2

No family is perfect and there are all sorts of things that family members can do to get on. Read the speech bubbles in Source 3 to see what other young people have suggested.

In small groups, write up a list of top tips for young people and adults who are living together as a family. Come up with at least five positive things that young people could do or say. Now find five things that adults could do or say. Think about why these are good examples and explain how they could help families to live in harmony. Here is an example:

Young people	Adults
1. I will walk the dog when it's my turn on the rota.	1. If you do what you agreed on the rota then I won't nag!

Activity 3

Imagine your family has been voted 'Family of the Year'. You have been chosen to go on stage and accept the award. Your acceptance speech must end with this sentence: 'In my family I would most like to thank … because …'.

Share your sentence with at least one other person in the class. Then when you get home, if you feel like it, share it there too!

Activity 4

Some people who have known each other for a really long time sometimes say they feel 'part of the family'. Sometimes joining a club, an activity or a religious group can also give us a 'family' to which we can belong. Who would you bring together in your ideal family household?

Don't be cheeky!

Try and get on – make compromises. That way you get somewhere.

Just be honest with your parents, because if you lie to them… well they know, and it doesn't really help.

My mum has a lot to cope with – the twins and me and my brother. But I do what I can to help, like washing up and stuff.

Just try not to fight with your brothers and sisters because that puts a strain on everything, especially your parents.

In this lesson you will:
- think about the roles and responsibilities of parents, carers and children in families
- consider how relationship skills can be built
- practise the social skill of appreciation within relationships.

Starter

Living together as a family involves everyone doing their share. Think of one thing that is your particular responsibility in your home, or a task that you always do. Explain what it is to your partner and whether you like doing it, or not!

Not everyone will like all the tasks that need to be done around the house. Should different members of a family have specific roles in the household? Look at how one family (who have one son and one daughter) share the various household responsibilities.

Task	Example family
Cleaning the kitchen	Dad helped by daughter sometimes
Cleaning the bathroom	Mum
Cooking	Dad
Doing the ironing	Dad – sometimes other family members help out
Tidying the living area(s)	Son and daughter
Tidying bedroom(s)	Each does their own
Looking after pets	Daughter
Domestic shopping (food and cleaning products)	Mum
Jobs outside the house: gardening, car washing	Dad and son

Source 1 Family life

Activity 1

1   Working as a group, either:
   a   complete the chart that your teacher will give you or
   b   draw up your own chart based on the tasks in Source 1.
   List who undertakes each task in *your* family.
2   Now think about how it was decided who would do each task in the first place and discuss the following questions in your group:
   - Did you choose your tasks, or were you told which tasks you had to do?
   - Do you think the distribution of tasks in your family is fair?
   - If you don't do your task, does another family member always end up doing it for you?

It's not just sharing out the tasks that can cause problems in a family. There can be all sorts of reasons for family rows and upsets.

Look at the things in Source 2 that families find help their communal life to run more smoothly.

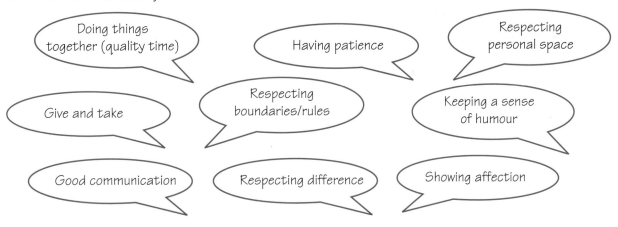

Doing things together (quality time)

Having patience

Respecting personal space

Give and take

Respecting boundaries/rules

Keeping a sense of humour

Good communication

Respecting difference

Showing affection

Source 2 Happy families?

Activity 2

1 Work together as a group and discuss the speech bubbles in Source 2. Construct a Diamond Nine by ranking each item in a diamond like the one below.

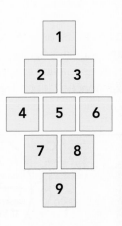

The item that you think is most important should go at the top and the one you think is the least important should be at the bottom. Make sure you discuss why you have ranked them in that order.

2 There are nine items in the speech bubbles. If you had to add a tenth one, what would it be?

The statements in the Diamond Nine all describe positive ways of getting along with each other, but when living communally, we can sometimes take each other for granted.

We might forget to thank a family member who helps us or whose company we really enjoy. Think about the people you live with. Is there someone who you would like to thank?

Thank you for the way you do the things you do

Way to go! **Well done!!!**

You are an inspiration

Source 3 Appreciation cards

Activity 3

1 Why might it sometimes be important to make the time to say thank you to the people who are around you everyday?
2 Look at the cards in Source 3 to give you ideas to make an appreciation card or poem that you could give to someone whose contribution to your life you value.

Activity 4

Apart from the tasks you undertake, what do you think your family members would say is the main contribution you make to family life?

8.4 How do I respond to other people?

In this lesson you will:
- learn about and practise some relationship skills
- practise the skills of communication and negotiation
- identify assertiveness skills.

Everyone has emotions and all sorts of things can trigger them. It's normal to experience a broad range of emotions during adolescence.

Whatever the emotions are – and however off-the-wall they might seem – they are very real when we experience them and therefore it is important to be aware of and to communicate our feelings. We also need to be responsible and learn to control our reactions when our emotions feel like they're taking over!

Starter

Our non-verbal communication is, for many of us, as important as the words we use. Think of two emotions you have felt today. In pairs, take turns to mime these two emotions to each other. Can your partner guess the two emotions you experienced? If not, try again.

One way of being direct and honest in any relationship is to use an 'I feel' statement. This is particularly effective when you're dealing with problems. See if you can spot the problem in Source 1.

Source 1 A problem

The situation in Source 1 could possibly have been turned around if, instead of shouting, the lender had explained how they felt. For example, 'When you didn't return my game for over two weeks I felt really angry and upset, because it's valuable and important to me and I haven't finished the game yet.'

This would have given the borrower a chance to admit they hadn't thought about how the lender felt and, at the same time, apologise.

Activity 1

In groups, look at the situations below and for each:
- come up with typical negative responses
- find ways to reach a positive solution with an 'I feel' statement.
  - **a** A friend ignores you.
  - **b** Your brother or sister borrows an item of clothing and doesn't return it.
  - **c** You do all of your chores at home but your parents doesn't thank you – they just give you even more to do.
  - **d** One of your grandparents (or another relation) teases you all the time in front of other people.
  - **e** A friend lies to you.
  - **f** A member of your family takes something of yours without asking.

Here's an example:

Situation	Typical negative response	'I feel' statement
A friend continually interrupts you.	Stop butting in. You are not the only one who wants to talk.	When you interrupt I feel hurt because I have something important to say too.

Sometimes we behave in certain ways because we don't want to risk spoiling a relationship. It is, however, important to be able to stand up for yourself and maintain relationships at the same time. The best way to do this is to be assertive. Some people get confused between aggressive and assertive behaviours. The differences are shown in Source 2.

Activity 2

Imagine a situation in which one person has spread some gossip about another.
- What words and actions would an aggressive person use to express how they feel?
- What words and actions would an assertive person use to express how they feel?

Activity 3

Look at the case studies your teacher will give you and, working in pairs, turn them into storyboards or comic strips. They must clearly describe, in words and pictures, a positive, assertive way to reach a solution that has a positive outcome for everyone. Remember how useful it is to include 'I feel' statements.

Activity 4

What personal behaviours could you work on so that you can stand up for what you believe in and care about?

Source 2 Aggressive or assertive?

Aggressive behaviour, as shown above, often includes shouting, pointing and invading someone's personal space. Aggressive language uses put-downs and insults.

Assertive behaviour, as shown above, often includes listening, speaking clearly and firmly without anger, respecting the other person and looking someone in the eye in a non-threatening way. Assertive language is honest without being hurtful.

8.5 How am I doing?

Starter

By now you will have covered many topics in PSHE. You may have learnt about:
- being healthy
- staying safe
- meeting and working with others
- managing money
- communicating confidently.

Think back over what you have covered and write down one or two key things you have enjoyed learning about.

In 2003 children and young people told the government that they wanted support to:
- be healthy
- stay safe
- enjoy and achieve
- make a positive contribution
- achieve economic wellbeing.

This became a big project called Every Child Matters (ECM): Change for Children. It involved everyone who worked with children and young people. This included teachers, doctors, nurses, social workers, youth workers and many other people.

ECM is all about making sure that children and young people can have a good life, whoever they are, and no matter what problems they may face.

Activity 1

It is really important that children and young people have a big say in the decisions that affect them. This PSHE course has been written to help you learn about things that are important in your lives and how they can affect you.

In your group, think back over what you have covered in PSHE and see if you can agree on one key thing that:

a you have learnt that was new to all of you

b you would like to learn more about

c enabled you to practise a useful skill.

Activity 2

The image of the tree in Source 1 depicts a person's good qualities, the skills they have developed and some of their short-term goals.
You will be given a copy of a tree to complete for yourself. Put your name in the centre of the tree. Think about how you will complete your tree to symbolise you. Work in pairs and discuss your trees to help each other decide what to put on them.

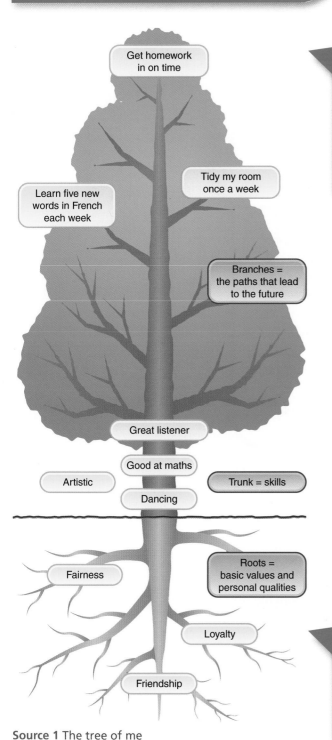

Activity 3

Working as a group of six, you will be given a sheet of five leaves to fill in as 'affirmations' of the other members of your group. Write the name of each person on a leaf, then write one thing that you really appreciate about them. Cut the leaves up and hand them in; your contributions will be anonymous.

Activity 4

You will be given the five leaves with your name on that were completed in Activity 3. Read these and then complete this sentence: 'The leaf I appreciate the most is the one that says … because …'.

Source 1 The tree of me

Get homework in on time

Tidy my room once a week

Learn five new words in French each week

Branches = the paths that lead to the future

Great listener

Good at maths

Artistic

Trunk = skills

Dancing

Fairness

Roots = basic values and personal qualities

Loyalty

Friendship

8.6 What are my rights and responsibilities?

In this lesson you will:
- learn that people have rights regardless of their different race, religion, culture, ability or disability, gender, age or sexual orientation
- research some of the rights that apply to you as a young person
- learn that every right comes with its own responsibility.

Starter

Why have people needed to make rules and laws to protect their rights as human beings? (Clue – think about freedom, protecting life and so on.) Can you think of any examples of laws that were made specifically to protect children and young people?

Activity 1

Since you've been born there have been some changes to laws in England. For instance, from 1 October 2007 shopkeepers have not been allowed to sell cigarettes to people under eighteen years of age. Why do you think this was law was made? How does this help to protect young people?

There are also laws and rules to make sure that you and others are not discriminated against. For example, only a short time ago all decisions in some schools were made by adults alone – there were no School Councils or other ways that pupils could voice their opinions.

When and where are there chances for you to get involved in rule-making in your school?

Article 12 – Children have the right to say what they think should happen, when adults are making decisions that affect them, and to have their opinions taken into account.

Article 15 – Children have the right to meet together and to join groups and organisations, as long as this does not stop other people from enjoying their rights.

Article 17 – Children have the right to reliable information from the mass media. Television, radio, and newspapers should provide information that children can understand, and should not promote materials that could harm children.

Source 1 UN rights

Activity 2

Look at the three rights that young people have in Source 1. These come from The United Nations Convention on the Rights of the Child. These rights are called 'Articles'. The United Kingdom has signed up to this Convention so they are your rights too.

Work in pairs to discuss one of these Articles. Come up with answers for these questions:

a   Do you think you and your friends get a real chance to exercise this right?

b   What might get in the way, or stop you fully benefiting from this right?

c   What do you think would have to change to make this right apply 100 per cent in your life?

You might want to research more information on the Convention of the Rights of the Child – there are 54 Articles! You can find out more at www.unicef.org/crc/files/Rights_overview.pdf.

Rights are extremely important. Without them we might have no education, be sent out to work for very low wages, work very long hours, have no freedom to choose what we could watch on TV or access on the internet.

So it's important to protect rights. One way of doing this is to remember that every right comes with a responsibility. Each person needs to get involved in protecting their rights and being responsible for other people's rights.

If children have a **right** to be protected from conflict, cruelty, exploitation and neglect, then they also have a **responsibility** not to bully or harm each other.

If children have a **right** to a clean environment, then they also have a **responsibility** to do what they can to look after their environment.

If children have a **right** to be educated, then they have the **obligation** to learn as much as their capabilities allow and, where possible, share their knowledge and experience with others.

Source 2 UN responsibilities

Activity 3

If you were a member of your School Council how would you ensure that the responsibilities in Source 2 were taken on by the pupils in your school?

Activity 4

How would you complete these sentences?
- 'As I get older I think an important right in my life will be …'
- 'I will balance this right with taking responsibility for …'

9.1 Who is in our communities?

In this lesson you will:
- learn about different groups in our communities
- appreciate some of the differences between people
- think about showing respect for other people's feelings.

Starter

Think of a word that describes you – the word must begin with the letter that begins your first name, for example: 'I am Jolly Jane'.

Activity 1

Look at the photos and the information box in Source 1. These photographs represent some of the variety of people in Britain today. Think about how you would answer these questions:

1 Were any people in the images familiar to you in any way? Did you recognise national or religious clothing, symbols, etc?
2 What differences did you notice?
3 What do all these people have in common?

In Britain people are protected from discrimination in different ways.

You should not be discriminated against in employment or the services you receive because:

- of your race or religious beliefs
- of your sexual orientation
- others think you are too old or too young
- you are male or female
- you are married or in a partnership
- you have a disability
- you have changed your gender
- you are pregnant.

Source 1 Variety and equality

Source 1 continued

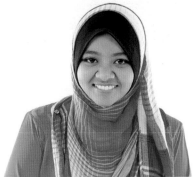

Activity 2

In pairs, draw a picture of each other. Don't worry about being a great artist, as you can add labels to describe what you have drawn. You can draw just head and shoulders or a whole body picture – it's up to you!

You will need to chat to each other as you do your drawings so that you can find out individual things about your partner.

For example, on the drawing you can label special points about the person, such as: shoe size 3, height 130cm, hair colour brown, eyes blue and so on.

Put the name of the person you have drawn at the top of the picture.

Activity 3

Now your task is to interview each other using the 'Who are you?' interview form your teacher will give you. This will cover a variety of likes and dislikes, such as favourite TV programmes, favourite food, pet or no pet, favourite pop group, and so on.

Include special things about the person that makes them unique. Choose two or three of the special things to add to the picture of this person that you drew in Activity 2. Look back at the photographs in Source 1 – some things were especially distinctive about each person. What positive things can you find about your partner that makes them unique?

Activity 4

You will probably have learnt a lot about several people in your class today. Now think about some things you have learnt about yourself during this activity.

What made you feel you are unique?

9.2 How do I feel about 'difference'?

In this lesson you will:
- reflect on 'difference' and what it means to individual people
- consider how prejudice might be challenged.

Starter

Look at Source 1. What do the photographs express about positive and negative views of 'difference'?

Source 1 Difference

We all know what it feels like to be different in one way or another. We know how uncomfortable and hurtful it can be if we are made to feel inferior because of that difference.

In the worst cases a fear and hatred of people who are different has led to events such as the Holocaust in the Second World War, 'ethnic cleansing' in the former Yugoslavia (1992), the genocide in Rwanda (1994) and to the humanitarian crisis in Darfur in the Sudan (2003). More recently, a civil war that had been going on for two decades, based chiefly on ethnic differences, ended in Sri Lanka (2009).

Recognising, understanding and accepting that there will always be similarities and differences between people may prevent ignorance, prejudice and fear from flourishing in the world.

Carmel

I liked my old school, but not my new school. In my old school I had lots of friends who were also black; in this school there are hardly any black people and none in my class. In lessons I feel OK, but I worry about break and dinner time when I get called all sorts of names. This is supposed to be a better school, but I don't like it and I want to go back to my old school.

Carmel is a young black woman.

Peter

Whenever people ridiculed somebody or something they called it 'gay'; people's trainers, music – even pencils – got called 'gay'. We were all supposed to think that anything gay must be bad. For almost a year of my school life, I spent every break and lunchtime sitting in the back of the library reading because I knew I was safe there, that I was isolated and no one would give me any hassle.

Peter is a young gay man.

Daniel

It was easy for me not to go to school. Mum and Dad worked and I often left the house after them and got back before them. They didn't know I was not going to school. I didn't do homework; the boys would take my bag off me when I got to school and throw the books about. When I didn't have my homework I couldn't tell the teacher it had been thrown away so I got into more trouble. It was better to stay at home.

Daniel has a learning disability.

Source 2 Feeling different

Activity 1

Read the three cases studies in Source 2 and, in pairs, discuss the following questions about one of them.
1. How would you feel if this happened to you?
2. Do you think the person in the case study has any options other than avoiding people? What are those options?
3. Is there any helpful advice you could give them?

First they came for the communists, and I did not speak out
because I was not a communist;
Then they came for the socialists, and I did not speak out
because I was not a socialist;
Then they came for the trade unionists, and I did not speak out
because I was not a trade unionist;
Then they came for the Jews, and I did not speak out
because I was not a Jew;
Then they came for me
and there was no one left to speak out for me.

Source 3 Not speaking out: A famous poem urging people to speak out against prejudice. It is attributed to Martin Niemöller, a prominent anti-Nazi German pastor.

Activity 3

Rewrite the poem in Source 3 in the context of today. What groups of people do you feel should be included now?

President Barack Obama

Activity 2

Read the poem in Source 3. It is a famous poem urging people to speak out against prejudice. It is attributed to Martin Niemöller, a prominent anti-Nazi German pastor. In speaking out against prejudice and hatred he was trying to make an important point. Answer the following questions:
1. What do you think is the central message of the poem?
2. Who are the 'they' mentioned in the poem?
3. What does the poem have to do with our lives at school?
4. Why is it important to defend other people's rights?

As individuals we each value different things. President Barack Obama has spoken about our common values. He said, 'the call to love one another; to understand one another; to treat with dignity and respect those with whom we share a brief moment on this Earth is the golden rule.'

Activity 4

What golden rule could you make that would express your values towards other people?

9.3 How can we value each other?

In this lesson you will:
• examine the communities that you belong to
• explore similarities and differences between yourself and others
• consider how you can learn about and value the similarities between people.

Starter

Your teacher will ask you to go and stand in a range of varying groups. Did anyone stay in the same group? It is important to remember that we are all different in many ways but that we also share things.

Source 1 Lee Mei and her communities

Source 1 depicts Lee Mei. She is a thirteen-year-old girl. As you can see, she belongs to a variety of communities:

- She is a member of the Lee family. (In Chinese culture the family name comes before the given (first) name.)
- She is a member of Year 8 at Springfield Community School.
- She lives in a semi-detached house in the Birchwood district of Lincoln.
- She and her mum, dad, grandfather, sister and brother are Buddhists.
- She is a British citizen and has a United Kingdom passport.

Even though people live their lives in different types of communities, we all share similar experiences. For example, everyone has a birthday; people have favourite or special foods; most people enjoy some kind of community celebration once a year; people mark special stages in their lives with parties and ceremonies and so on.

Source 2 is an example of individual people who although they may appear 'different' actually share important similarities with each other.

Activity 2

Look at Source 2. These two women both won gold medals in London in 2012 and were both awarded OBEs. Can you think of other ways in which people who appear different at first glance, may share similarities?

Activity 3

Work together in a small group and discuss the following topics – see if you share any similarities across the whole group.
- One festival/celebration that you all take part in
- One healthy food that you all enjoy eating
- One achievement you've all experienced since joining this school
- One badge/charity bracelet that you would all be proud to wear

Activity 4

Complete this sentence: 'I share … with the entire human race and I am also unique and special because … '

Activity 1

Everyone belongs to more than one community. Draw a diagram either like Lee Mei's in Source 1 or of your own design to represent you and the different communities to which you belong.

Source 2 Gold medal winners

Charlotte Dujardin was awarded an OBE after winning two gold medals for dressage at the London Olympics 2012.

Sophie Christiansen was awarded an OBE after winning three gold medals in equestrian events at the London Paralympics 2012.

9.4 What makes a successful community?

Starter

We each belong to a number of communities, for example our neighbourhood; our family; our school; perhaps a religious or cultural community; and we are all citizens of a very large community – the United Kingdom.

Name four communities that you belong to and, for each one, identify something you enjoy or benefit from by being part of that community.

Think back over your PSHE lessons, and possibly other lessons too: you may have negotiated a Group Agreement based on rights and responsibilities. This was a type of 'community contract' where you gained rights and at the same time contributed by taking on responsibilities.

Activity 1

Source 1 shows individuals looking after their community. Each of us individually gains from being part of a community – and there are things we already do (or should be doing) so that other members of the community benefit as well. Take one of your example communities from the Starter activity and list three things you gain from being part of that community and three things you contribute to it.

Source 1 Looking after the community

Imagine a futuristic experiment which involves setting up a colony of earth (Novo-Earth) on a new planet (see Source 2). A representative selection of people from across the world has been chosen to take part in this new community. They include people with the variety of skills needed to set up a society, for example teachers, doctors, engineers and so on. You are among the teenagers included. Everyone has a vital role to play and has been chosen because they are able to contribute to this new community.

Source 2 Life in the new community of Novo-Earth

The people of Novo-Earth will need to set up rules and guidelines to live by. Although these people come from many different countries on Earth, they all share Earth's Universal Declaration of Human Rights. As part of the consultation process you have been invited to put forward three rules or guidelines that uphold some of the Human Rights in the Declaration.

Activity 2

1 In groups, work on one of the categories below:
   - Education
   - Health and wellbeing
   - Equality
   - Employment
   - Freedom of thought/belief
2 Read the articles on pages 130–1: The Universal Declaration of Human Rights – some selected articles.
3 For your allocated category, use your own words to explain three rules or guidelines for Novo-Earth that you think uphold some of the relevant points in the Universal Declaration of Human Rights.
4 Give feedback on your three points to the rest of the class.
5 Individually decide on which of the points in each category is the most important and take a class vote to decide the top guideline in each category. This should give you five key rules/guidelines for the new community.

Not all of the rules we live by are written down. Culturally, many groups have evolved informal ways of behaving that encourage harmony, for example being courteous, respecting people who are different, helping neighbours, and so on.

Activity 3

Look back at Source 1. Leaving laws and guidelines aside, what ways of behaving would you like to see that would promote harmony and wellbeing?

Activity 4

Sometimes people talk about living by their 'golden rule', for example 'Treat other people as you would like to be treated'. Communities could benefit from a golden rule too. What would be your golden rule for a community to live by and why?

The Universal Declaration of Human Rights: selected articles

Article 1
All human beings are born free and equal in dignity and rights. They are endowed with reason and conscience and should act towards one another in a spirit of brotherhood.

Article 2
Everyone is entitled to all the rights and freedoms set forth in this Declaration, without distinction of any kind, such as race, colour, sex, language, religion, political or other opinion, national or social origin, property, birth or other status.

Article 3
Everyone has the right to life, liberty and security of person.

Article 4
No one shall be held in slavery or servitude; slavery and the slave trade shall be prohibited in all their forms.

Article 5
No one shall be subjected to torture or to cruel, inhuman or degrading treatment or punishment.

Article 6
Everyone has the right to recognition everywhere as a person before the law.

Article 7
All are equal before the law and are entitled without any discrimination to equal protection of the law.

Article 8
Everyone has the right to an effective remedy by the competent national tribunals for acts violating the fundamental rights granted him by the constitution or by law.

Article 9
No one shall be subjected to arbitrary arrest, detention or exile.

Article 10
Everyone is entitled in full equality to a fair and public hearing by an independent and impartial tribunal, in the determination of his rights and obligations and of any criminal charge against him.

Article 11
Everyone charged with a penal offence has the right to be presumed innocent until proved guilty according to law in a public trial at which he has had all the guarantees necessary for his defence.

Article 12
No one shall be subjected to arbitrary interference with his privacy, family, home or correspondence, nor to attacks upon his honour and reputation. Everyone has the right to the protection of the law against such interference or attacks.

Article 13
(1) Everyone has the right to freedom of movement and residence within the borders of each state.
(2) Everyone has the right to leave any country, including his own, and to return to his country.

Article 14
Everyone has the right to seek and to enjoy in other countries asylum from persecution.

Article 15
Everyone has the right to a nationality.

Article 16
Men and women of full age, without any limitation due to race, nationality or religion, have the right to marry and to found a family.

Article 17
Everyone has the right to own property alone as well as in association with others.

Article 18
Everyone has the right to freedom of thought, conscience and religion.

Article 19
Everyone has the right to freedom of opinion and expression.

Article 20
Everyone has the right to freedom of peaceful assembly and association.

Article 21
(1) Everyone has the right to take part in the government of his country, directly or through freely chosen representatives.

(2) Everyone has the right of equal access to public service in his country.

Article 22
Everyone, as a member of society, has a right to social security.

Article 23
(1) Everyone has the right to work, to free choice of employment, to just and favourable conditions of work and to protection against unemployment.
(2) Everyone, without any discrimination, has the right to equal pay for equal work.
(3) Everyone who works has the right to just and favourable remuneration.
(4) Everyone has the right to form and to join trade unions for the protection of his interests.

Article 24
Everyone has the right to rest and leisure, including reasonable limitation of working hours and periodic holidays with pay.

Article 25
Everyone has the right to a standard of living adequate for the health and wellbeing of himself and of his family, including food, clothing, housing and medical care and necessary social services, and the right to security in the event of unemployment, sickness, disability, widowhood, old age or other lack of livelihood in circumstances beyond his control.

Article 26
Everyone has the right to education.

Article 27
(1) Everyone has the right to freely participate in the cultural life of the community, to enjoy the arts and to share in scientific advancement and its benefits.
(2) Everyone has the right to the protection of the moral and material interests resulting from any scientific, literary or artistic production of which he is the author.

Article 28
Everyone is entitled to a social and international order in which the rights and freedoms set forth in this Declaration can be fully realised.

9.5 What can cause problems in communities?

In this lesson you will:
- consider problems from more than one point of view
- learn about the importance of talking and negotiating in solving problems
- look at the role of mediation in problem-solving.

Starter

Most people live happily together in their communities but sometimes things go wrong. What sorts of problems can arise between people who live in the same community?

The problems that arise in communities may often have more than one cause. There may be a particular incident or problem that has cropped up but also people's underlying feelings can make a situation more difficult. For example, if people feel angry, frightened or threatened they may respond in a way that makes the situation worse.

Source 1 Hanging out together

Activity 1

Look at the photograph in Source 1. It shows a group of young people who regularly gather together on one of the streets of a residential neighbourhood. Several residents are unhappy about the young people meeting like this.
1 What do you think the residents are concerned about?
2 What feelings might the residents have that might make the situation flare up?
3 How do you think a resolution might be reached?

Activity 2

Look at the situations described in Source 2. Working in groups, answer the following questions for one of the situations:
1 What reasonable point could either side raise to explain their concerns?
2 What feelings might each side be experiencing?
3 What negotiations and compromises would be necessary for the characters to achieve an outcome where both feel happier?

Source 2 Problems, problems, problems

Anna

You are an enthusiastic amateur gardener keen on self-sufficiency and 'green' issues. You rented an allotment earlier this year and are growing your own fruit and veg. You won't use weedkiller and you work hard to keep your patch clear of weeds. You enjoy the friendly atmosphere between the different allotment holders and look forward to your weekly visits. However, you are concerned that George's weeds are creeping into your plot and killing your plants.

George

Your allotment is next to Anna's. You've had it for years and don't worry too much about weeds and creepers – as long as you can grow flowers and a few seasonal vegetables to take home to the family you are happy. Recently you haven't been able to visit as often as you'd like since your back has started playing up. Things are getting a bit out of hand on your allotment but you don't consider it a big problem.

Jay

You are fourteen years old and your parents have split up. You are happy at your present school and have lots of friends there. Your dad and his new partner have moved to the next town – about five miles away. Your mum is staying in the house where you all lived together and wants you to live with her. Your school is half way between the two homes so whatever happens you won't need to move schools. You'd like to spend your time equally with both parents – but they're angry with each other and won't discuss things.

Jon

You are Jay's father. You and your wife have split up after being together for sixteen years. You have had to move out of the home you all shared. You really miss Jay and would like it if Jay came to live with you. You feel really upset about the situation. Your ex-wife is angry with you and won't allow you back in the house. She completely blames you for the breakdown of the relationship. She doesn't want to speak to you.

Niquil

You are the middle child of a family of three children aged nine to fifteen. You live with your dad on the sixth floor of a block of flats in the Derwent Estate. You like to play in the street and to ride your bike on the pavement, where it feels safer than on the road. Your dad is happy for you to play outside until he gets home from work or it gets dark.

Sam

You are retired and live alone in a house with its own garden on the Derwent Estate. You like to go for a walk at least once a day but don't feel as steady on your feet as you used to. You enjoy having families around you, they liven up the neighbourhood, but you are worried about being knocked over by children riding their bikes on the pavement and playing in the street.

Mediation

One way that community or family disputes can be resolved is by a process called mediation. You may already have come across pupil mediation services in school, which sometimes deal with issues such as bullying. Here are just three examples of services that can help provide advice and/or mediation when things go wrong:

- Some local councils have a mediation service to resolve disputes between neighbours.
- The Citizens Advice Bureau can provide useful advice to anyone with a problem.
- Independent mediation services or charities are often used by families who are experiencing problems.

Activity 3

Look at the information in Source 3. Discuss what situations in school and your other communities might be helped if mediation was available.

Source 3 Mediation

What is mediation?

Mediation is a way of dealing with disputes which helps people to reach an agreement that everyone is satisfied with.

Mediation does not judge or blame people but tries to help people work towards an agreement for the future.

Mediation helps all the issues to be heard and understood. It may be that some of the people involved do not realise that there is a problem.

How does mediation work?

The mediators will listen to what each person has to say and help them to explore the options available.

The mediator will not tell the people what to do but will help them to reach an agreement.

9.6 How can I contribute to my community?

In this lesson you will:
- look at community services and who provides them
- consider how volunteers contribute to their communities
- think about ways in which you could contribute to your community.

Starter

Your local authority will have an obligation to provide a range of services. Do you know what those services are?

In British communities, services are provided by various groups, for example, the local authority (council), the National Health Service (NHS), the police, national charities and agencies such as the Samaritans, local charities and voluntary community groups.

Activity 1

Here are problems that a community might face:
- A busy road with no pedestrian crossing
- Nowhere for children to play
- An elderly person who is cold and lonely.

Who should put these things right and why should it be up to them to do so?

The UK Government encourages voluntary groups to provide a wide range of services in local communities. Visitors to the UK often remark on our strong tradition of voluntary and community support. An example of this is given in Source 1, a case study of Aghalee Village Hall in Northern Ireland, which won the Queen's Award for Voluntary Service.

Activity 2

Read the case study in Source 1 on page 136. Imagine that you have been given a building that comprises a main hall, several meeting rooms, a kitchen and lavatories, and grounds around the building that can be used for a variety of activities. The facility has comprehensive disabled access.

You need to run this community venue for the benefit of as many groups as possible.

1 Which groups do you already know about in your community who could use this venue?
2 Using the case study in Source 1 for ideas, what range of activities would you introduce to attract other members of the community to use your venue?

Source 1 Aghalee Village Hall

Case study

Aghalee Village Hall Management Committee has run the village hall for over 70 years, providing local residents with a focal point for their social, educational and sporting activities. Every day some activity takes place in the hall, including Tiny Tots Playgroup, a club for the elderly, dog training classes, junior ballet, a junior sports club, a badminton club, local art classes and Alcoholics Anonymous meetings. The local Development Association also hold their monthly meetings in the hall.

The two biggest events that the Management Committee run are the annual Children's Sports and Fun Day, which is followed by a barbecue and dance in the hall; and the annual Lighting of the Christmas Tree with a visit by Father Christmas.

Many community groups pay to use the hall. This income is largely used to pay for the maintenance and upkeep of the hall. On Friday evenings the hall has become increasingly popular for private functions and birthday parties for both the young and the old – this is another way of raising funds to keep the hall safe and weather-proof.

Since 1933 the hall has been run by volunteers who are elected at the AGM. The Committee is representative of all the user groups and members of the local community. One of the major concerns of the Committee is to keep the village hall in as good a state of repair as possible in order that it will continue to be appreciated by all the user groups. (Aghalee Village Hall Management Committee, Lisburn, N. Ireland)

People in Aghalee recently celebrated the 80th anniversary of running their community venue on a voluntary basis. Think of the thousands of voluntary hours that members of the community have donated to help this project and each other.

Here are some of the ways in which members of the community contributed their time:

- Accounting and running the finances
- Cleaning
- Cooking and serving meals
- Fundraising
- Gardening and maintenance of the grounds
- Keeping the bookings diary
- Keeping the building well maintained and safe
- Liaising with the local council
- Marketing what the facility offers
- Painting and decorating
- Running courses/classes
- Secretarial work

Aghalee keeps its successful community links strong by using social networking as well as activities at the hall.

Activity 3

Look at the list of activities that you generated in Activity 2 and the list of tasks the volunteers at Aghalee undertake. Answer the following questions:

1 Which class or activity could you help to teach or run?
2 Which tasks could you contribute to?
3 What qualities do you think you have to offer your community?

While you are still at school it won't necessarily be easy or appropriate to commit a lot of time to volunteering. However, many people your age do contribute to their communities in different ways.

For example, Community Service Volunteers (CSV) is a volunteering and learning charity in the UK that offers information on how young people can get involved. Its Young Voices project, which ran until 2010, aimed to get young people to volunteer in public libraries. This encouraged more young people to use the library and learn new skills. CSV is currently supporting 'Step Up To Serve' (www. stepuptoserve.org.uk), which aims to double the number of people aged 10–20 taking part in social action – that is, practical action in the service of others – by 2020.

Activity 4

What do you do that makes a positive contribution to your community?

In this lesson you will:
- research information about some of the leading agencies that support young people
- present that information to others in the form of a case study.

Samaritans is a well-known national agency that provides help and support. What sort of service do they offer? Who can use their service?

Samaritans

We don't know when you might need us.
That's why we are open 24 hours a day.

The aim of the agency

Samaritans provides confidential non-judgemental emotional support, 24 hours a day for people who are experiencing feelings of distress or despair, including those which could lead to suicide. Samaritans say: 'Whatever you're going through, whether it's big or small, don't bottle it up. We are here for you if you're worried about something, feel upset or confused, or just want to talk to someone.'

The service it offers

People can contact them for support by telephone, email, letter and face to face in most of their branches. Samaritans is available to anyone in the UK and Ireland.

Samaritans is run by

It is a national charity with local branches and local volunteers in most major towns and cities.

Information on their website includes

Details about problems such as depression and how people can be helped; how to volunteer and support Samaritans; contact details for email and local services.

An example of someone who was helped by the Samaritans

'One night, around 2am, I phoned Samaritans. A young woman spoke to me but I just didn't know what to say. I couldn't talk about what was happening. So she asked me what I'd done that day and gradually I was able to tell her my story. As I was talking I began to feel a sense of relief as it all came out. When I came off the phone after an hour I was overwhelmed by a feeling of peace and was able to go straight to sleep. It helped so much that I called back the following night. I spoke to a few different volunteers over the next two weeks. It was the same story every night; I just needed to tell someone about it all. They were brilliant, absolutely brilliant. After I phoned Samaritans, I felt more able to get on with my life. After six months ... I felt I could cope.'

People can get in touch with Samaritans to find out more by:
- Phoning 08457 909090 (your local branch number will be in your local directory)
- Sending an email to jo@samaritans.org

Source 1 A case study of a helping agency

When Samaritans was first set up, there were few agencies that specifically helped young people – today all that has changed. Samaritans is just one of many voluntary agencies that offer help to people when they need someone to turn to. The next activity will look at agencies that particularly support young people.

Activity 1

1 Look at Source 2, which shows five agencies that help young people. Your teacher will allocate you one of these agencies and ask you to work with other pupils in a small group. Your task will be to do research, assemble information and present a case study about one of these agencies. Each one of them could be invaluable to you or other pupils in the future – so this case study could provide crucial awareness of the sort of support that is available to someone who is facing a crisis or a difficult time.

You could present your case study as a:
- magazine or newspaper article
- talk with PowerPoint illustrations
- radio or television interview, with some members of your group as interviewers and others as members of the organisation.

In your group remember to plan your work by deciding roles and responsibilities for undertaking various parts of the case study (for example, research, creating the presentation slides, speakers, background music).

Whatever your format, as in the Samaritans example in Source 1, ensure your case study includes:
- the main aim of the agency
- the services it offers to young people
- who runs it (for example, a charity or a government department)
- details of the sort of information you can get online
- an example of someone who received help
- details of how people can get in touch with the agency or find out more.

2 After each group's presentation you may want to offer your feedback. Try to identify:
- at least one thing your group liked about the presentation content
- at least one thing your group liked about the presentation style
- one thing that your group thinks could have improved the presentation content
- one thing that your group thinks could have improved the presentation style.

Source 2 Five helping agencies

Anti-bullying Alliance www.anti-bullyingalliance.org.uk	
Childline www.childline.org.uk	
a kidspace www.akidspace.co.uk	
Think U Know www.thinkuknow.co.uk	
YoungMinds www.youngminds.org.uk/ for_children_young_people	

Activity 2

If you could invite someone from one of these agencies to come in to school and talk to pupils, which agency would you invite? Why?

9.8 How can we challenge prejudice and discrimination?

In this lesson you will:
- find out what 'prejudice' and 'discrimination' mean
- think about different types of prejudice
- consider how to challenge prejudice and discrimination assertively.

Starter

Look at the photographs in Source 1. They are what you would probably see and experience in any local town or city. They don't present a challenge to the majority of people, but they could cause problems for others. Who do you think might have difficulties and why?

People who have particular needs or disabilities can find that their needs are not taken into consideration when moving around town. Worse still, other people may decide they know what's best for someone else.

> Prejudice means pre-judging people based on what a person thinks they know about them. For example, some older people might think that teenagers hanging around in their local shopping centre *must* be up to no good, even if they aren't.

All sorts of people may experience prejudice because others don't bother to get to know them, or check if their opinion of that person is actually the truth.

Activity 1

What sorts of prejudice might the following people experience from others in our society?
1 A person with visual impairment (blind person)
2 A person who uses a wheelchair to get around
3 A person who cannot read or speak English
4 A teenage 'hoodie'
5 A person who looks different from the majority of people around them because of the clothes they are wearing or the way they wear their hair

Prejudice can lead to people being discriminated against.

> Discrimination means treating somebody differently because of something about them. Source 2 shows some words that describe different types of prejudice.

Source 1 In and around town

Source 2 Types of prejudice

Ageism

Sexism

Racism

Homophobia

Activity 2

What types of prejudice do the words in Source 2 refer to? In groups, come up with a definition for one of the terms and give examples of how this prejudiced attitude could lead to somebody being discriminated against.

Activity 3

Imagine your local newspaper has recently published a series of articles about prejudice and discrimination in the community.

Choose one of the newspaper headlines in Source 3 and write a letter to the editor explaining why you think this prejudice needs to be challenged.

When writing your letter you will need to include comments about how a person can suffer prejudice in the:
- language used towards them
- way others behave towards them
- jokes or comments made about them.

Fit and healthy but too old to be on lollipop patrol

Woman 'brickie' told to put up with the lads' wolf whistles

Insulting graffiti sprayed in Jewish cemetery

Woman told 'You can't use the ladies room because you used to be a man'

Hotel owners refuse room to gay couple

Source 3 Newspaper headlines

Activity 4

If you could do one simple thing to challenge prejudice, what would it be and how would you do it?

10.1 How do I work best with others?

In this lesson you will learn:
- that people have multiple roles and responsibilities in society
- to think about how different roles help make a group successful
- why positive relationships are helpful when working in groups.

Starter

Each of us has many roles in life. Look at the picture of Ajit and the number of different roles he has in Source 1. There are probably many more that aren't even listed. Think of yourself: what roles do you have in your life?

Source 1 This is Ajit. Ajit is ...

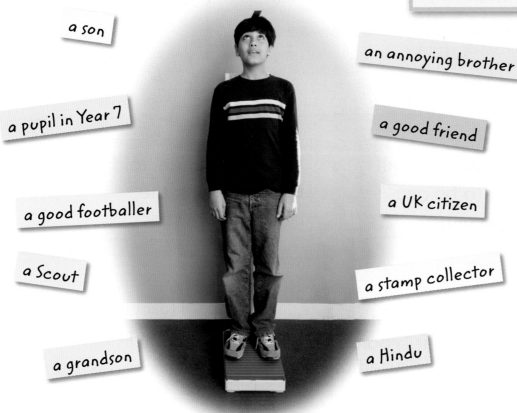

a son

an annoying brother

a pupil in Year 7

a good friend

a good footballer

a UK citizen

a Scout

a stamp collector

a grandson

a Hindu

Activity 1

This competition is to see which group can build the tallest tower.
1 Each group must have exactly the same number and size of sheets of newspaper, and a roll of sticky tape.
2 You are not allowed to fix your tower to any surface in the room – it must be freestanding.
3 Each group is only allowed ten minutes to build their tower from newspaper and sticky tape!

Learning about what you do best and what motivates you starts at school. There is no job where you work entirely on your own. You will always be working with other people, even if it's via a phone or a computer. So it's important to take other people's skills and attitudes into account.

Skills are things that you have learnt to help you do a job well, such as organising or writing notes and lists.

Attitudes are the personal characteristics and behaviours you display, such as reliability in turning up for a job.

Both are important in school and the workplace.

Source 2 Successful group work depends on recognising different attitudes.

Activity 2

Sometimes working in a group or team isn't a happy experience. Things go wrong or the group just doesn't seem to gel.
Working in pairs, list all the reasons that get in the way of a team being happy and successful. Think about actions, words and attitudes.

Activity 3

1 What jobs, paid and unpaid, do pupils in your class currently do?
2 What skills and attitudes are required for each job?

Activity 4

1 Look at Source 2 showing eight people at a meeting.
Match the feelings below to the faces:
 a bossiness
 b boredom
 c shyness
 d frustration
 e confusion
 f eagerness
 g nervousness
 h involvement
2 In groups, discuss what it's like to work with other people.
 • Compare how you feel and behave when you work in a) large groups, b) in pairs and c) on your own.
 • What skills and attitudes are useful for a), b) and c)? Are different skills required?
 • Which skills and attitudes do members need to develop for successful group work?

Activity 5

What is your best attitude or skill that you can bring to a team?

In this lesson you will learn:
- about good listening skills
- to practise speaking and listening to others
- to identify ways that good listening can help you and other people.

Starter

Choose a subject that you think you could talk about for 'Just a Minute'. It can be anything that interests you or you feel you know a lot about: for example a hobby, a famous person, a sport or your favourite subject.

In pairs, talk for one minute each on your chosen topic. Try not to repeat yourself, pause too much or end up talking about something else.

Take turns and time the other person. How easy was it for each of you to talk for one minute?

Activity 1

In the Starter activity you were probably concentrating on being a good speaker – but how good a listener were you?

1 Without help from your partner:
   a Write down the three most important facts or ideas you thought you heard while *they* were speaking.
   b Write down the three most important facts or ideas that you think *you* spoke about.
   c Read your lists to each other – do they agree? Were you a good listener to what your partner was saying?

   Sometimes we need to practise listening as much as speaking.

2 Work together in your pair to identify up to five things that make somebody a good listener. Then explain them to the rest of your class.

Listening skills assessment levels

4 'Active Listening' – you are paying attention to what they say and how they say it: their feelings about the subject.

3 'Hearing the Content' – you are taking in basic facts, opinions and so on.

2 'Superficial Listening' – you are going through the motions of listening but aren't really paying attention.

1 'Ignoring' – you know the other person is talking but you are not responding to them.

Source 1

Activity 2

Work with a different person in a pair and play the 'Just a Minute' activity again.

This time, when you are the listener, choose one of the Listening Skill levels in Source 1 and play the role of someone listening at that level. See if your partner can guess which Listening Skill level you were demonstrating.

Source 2 Talking with others

Teachers

Family members

Shop assistants

One of the emergency services

Activity 3

Obviously it feels good when someone is really listening to us. In what situations is it important to be a good listener when talking with others?

Work in a small group to come up with examples where being a good listener is vital when you are communicating with the people in Source 2.

Activity 4

Complete this sentence: 'My top tip for being a really good listener is …'.

10.3 What do I want and how do I get it?

In this lesson you will learn:
- to think about the positive things you want in the future
- to create steps to help you achieve your goals
- how to turn steps into targets.

Starter

Is it easier to work towards a goal that you have set for yourself, or one that has been set for you by someone else?

Activity 1

Sheryl (Source 1) lives in a happy neighbourhood and knows other people in her street, joins in local activities and helps her mum serve tea at the local senior citizens' Friendship Club.

She wants to go on her school's Year 7 trip to France because she enjoyed the same trip when she was at primary school. Her parents say that the primary school trip was less than a year ago and she has had a family holiday since then. They tell her they only feel able to contribute 50 per cent of the cost of this trip – but if she can raise the other 50 per cent, she can go.

- What steps can Sheryl take to raise the rest of the money?
- What can she do on her own?
- Will she need to work with other people?
- In what way might she need other support from adults?

Source 1 Sheryl

Activity 2

In the Starter activity you began to look at the reasons for setting your own personal goals. This activity gives you the chance to practise setting goals by working out steps to help someone solve a problem.

- On her way to school Tracy regularly sees Archie. She would like to become friends with him. They have never had a real conversation with each other but they recognise and smile at each other, and nod 'hello'.
  Tracy's goal: To become friends with Archie.

- Daniel's younger brother and sister really irritate him, and he tends to lose his temper when they are around. He knows that he has said hurtful things to them and would really like to be able to control his temper.
  Daniel's goal: To control his temper when he's around his brother and sister.

- Hari is having real difficulties in one of her subjects. She wants to improve her chances to do better. Her teacher is willing to help but points out she has fallen behind her homework schedule. Hari has several pieces of overdue homework in more than one subject, and doesn't know where to start.
  Hari's goal: To improve her study skills.

Discuss solutions for these people, using the Goal Setting Planner your teacher will give you.

In Activity 2 you helped other people by breaking their goals down into achievable steps and finding solutions to blocks in their way.

We sometimes call these steps 'targets'. You may have already been setting targets at school, or perhaps this idea is new to you.

The targets you set have to be achievable, not just a hope or a wish. The best way of setting a target is to think of them as SMART targets:

S   Specific, for example, I will improve the presentation of my work by always putting the date and underlining titles. Not – I will make my work look better.

M   Measurable, for example, I will improve my punctuality to 100 percent this term. Not – I will try to be on time.

A   Attainable, for example, I will attend choir club every week. Not – I will sing the solo in the next school concert.

R   Realistic, for example, I will learn 10 new words in Spanish each week. Not – I will learn 50 new words in Spanish each day.

T   Time-specific, for example, I will aim to achieve these targets by the next half-term holiday. Not – I will do this as soon as I can.

Source 2 SMART targets

Activity 3

Here are some goals written by pupils your age. Turn them into SMART targets. Use Source 2 to help you work out which bit of S-M-A-R-T to use for each one.
- I'll get completely up to date with my homework.
- I'll try to visit my auntie more often.
- I must improve my piano playing.
- I am going to keep my bedroom tidy all the time.
- I'll get round to my revision before the exams start.

Activity 4

How could you apply the SMART target idea to something you want to achieve in your own life?

10.4 How do I plan for my future?

In this lesson you will learn:
- about the meaning of the word 'career'
- what careers might suit you in the future
- how you might begin to plan a career.

Starter

Most people want to achieve things in life, but get distracted from their goals. You can stay focused by coming up with your own personal motto. For example, somebody who is good at putting things off could use the motto 'Do it now!'

What personal motto would help keep you focused on your goals?

Activity 1

Is there a difference between doing a job and having a career? Look at the list in Source 1, and decide whether you think each person is doing a job or having a career.

- Actor
- Newsreader
- Newsagent
- Nurse
- Paperboy/ papergirl
- Parent

- Pop star
- Postman/ postwoman
- Professional footballer
- Shop assistant
- Soldier

- Supermarket checkout assistant
- Teacher
- Traffic warden
- Vet
- Window cleaner

Source 1 Career or job?

Activity 2

Pupils in Year 7 told us that when they hear the question 'What do you want to do when you grow up?' they want to say things like:
- 'Give it a rest, I'm only eleven!'
- 'I don't know.'
- 'Be an astronaut.'
- 'Not a lot.'
- 'Be famous.'
- 'I haven't really thought about it.'

Of course, you might have thought about it … but then again maybe you haven't. No one should feel under pressure to make such a big decision at this stage in life. You will change a lot as you grow up, and new sorts of jobs and careers could be available in the future.

However, thinking about your personal strengths and interests can help you start the journey.

Make a spider diagram like the one in Source 2, with you at the centre and all the things you're good at and your interests around you. Spend some quiet time seeing where your diagram takes you.

Source 2 What I'm good at and what I enjoy doing

Activity 3

Even the most glamorous of careers will have a tedious side to it. There will always be routines that need to be followed and qualifications that need to be gained.

Let's think about the example of a soldier from Activity 1. The recruitment adverts usually show them on active duty (hiding in forests, climbing mountains, jumping out of planes – all looking very exciting!), but Source 3 lists some of the practical things a soldier needs to learn to do.

What would be the practical tasks and routines that each of the following would have to do?

- Member of a boy/girl band
- Someone running a pub
- Fitness instructor at a gym
- Dancer in a musical
- Cosmetic surgeon
- On-board crew for an airline
- Nanny in a celebrity family
- Morning TV presenter

1   Be awake, up and ready to work at a specific time.

2   Follow set routines for preparing your uniform.

3   Tidy your living area.

4   Clean your equipment.

5   Practise drill and exercise routines.

6   Develop teamwork skills.

7   Take responsibility for specific tasks.

Source 3 Being a soldier

Activity 4

Complete the following sentence:
'When I leave school, a statement I would like to read about myself in my school record is …'.

10.5 What do I need to plan for?

In this lesson you will learn:
- how we think about our abilities and how others regard our abilities
- about self-confidence and getting to know ourselves
- how to get the tools for a successful future
- the importance of thinking about the future today.

Starter

How do you see yourself?
- 'Do it now' person
- 'Wait and see' person
- 'Think, plan and take action' person
- 'Take opportunities as they present themselves' person
- 'Head in the clouds' person

Compare notes with the person next to you.

Are they surprised by how you see yourself?

At some point in your life someone has probably told you off for only thinking about yourself or being selfish. They might have had a point!

However, believing in yourself isn't always a selfish or bad thing. Belief in yourself, or self-confidence, is a vital tool in life.

Activity 1

1 Think about five positive things that describe the sort of person you think you are. Now think about the points you might like to change about yourself. Copy and complete the table below.

Positive points about the way I am now	Things about myself I want to change

2 How confident do you feel about changing? As a class, discuss what holds people back from being what they want to be.

Imagine the biggest and best luxury liner sailing across a calm sea. What do you think will happen if the mechanism for steering – the rudder – breaks? Your mind and willpower are your rudder. They steer you towards your destination.

Think about what sort of life you might like. For instance, do you want a career that allows you to:

● travel
● earn lots of money
● spend time with your family
● meet lots of interesting people
● help people
● follow a special interest?

Now consider what would happen if you didn't give your life or career any thought at all. Without plans, most people will drift eventually. If you want to succeed at something you enjoy, you need to think and make decisions about what you want to do.

Whatever you decide to do in life, in order to get there you need basic skills in various areas, such as those shown in Source 1. Plan to succeed by working towards developing these basics skills.

Source 1 Getting the basics right

Punctuality   Appearance   Attitude   Written communication   Spoken communication

Activity 2

1 Jim is going for an interview for a job as an estate agent. Look at the first column of the table below. How could Jim show these skills to make a good impression on the person interviewing him? Then, consider what would make the interviewer think twice before considering Jim for the job. Copy and complete the table:

Areas in which skills are required	What creates a good impression?	What creates a bad impression?
Punctuality		
Appearance *(dressing appropriately)*		
Attitude		
Written communication *(think about what would make a good impression if you are filling in a form)*		
Spoken communication *(how you talk and what you say in answer to questions)*		

2 Discuss whether you think the expression 'You only have one chance to make a first impression' is true.

Activity 3

The Latin expression, *carpe diem* means 'seize the day' or 'do it now'. As a class, discuss why today is a good time to start thinking about your future.

10.6 What opportunities are out there for me?

In this lesson you will:
- consider factors that may motivate your career choices
- think more widely about your future career
- find out where to look for information about careers
- plan for the future with confidence.

Source 1 Motivating factors

a) Money

b) Prospects (whether you are likely to be able to progress steadily with this career, gaining more responsibility and money)

c) Satisfaction

d) Location (where the career is situated)

e) Flexibility

f) Suitability (whether you have the necessary talents and skills)

Starter

1. Look at the factors in Source 1. They might influence your choice of career. Put them in order of importance – with 1 being most important and 6 least important.
2. Which factors scored most highly in your class?
3. Taken in isolation, should any of these factors alone determine your career choice?

It is very important to think about your skills, interests and qualities when choosing a future career as well as the financial rewards it might bring. This is because enjoying what you do will make your life happier.

Sometimes people end up being influenced into careers that other people think they should do. It's important to avoid being pigeonholed into a career just because you are male or female. For example, on TV, most doctors are portrayed chiefly as men and nurses as women; male actors often play lawyers, women play bar staff or cleaners. Don't let stereotypes stop you!

Activity 1

1 Catherine has no idea what she wants to do when she 'grows up', but she is organised, likes researching projects and is good at maths.
List five different careers that might suit her talents.
2 As a class, discuss how Catherine's career choices broaden if we take into account that she loves animals and is a caring member of the class.

With so many careers open to you, it might be easy for you to decide not to think about it – after all, you have so much time.

In fact, it is not only exciting thinking about the future but it is never too early to give this subject a little of your attention. Believe it or not, it will help a lot later on.

Source 2 Catherine

Activity 2

1 Look at Source 3. Think about the skills and attitudes that are presented. Now, draw your own spider diagram with you in the centre. At the end of each line, write or illustrate something that you are good at. Take time to look carefully at this information. What conclusions can you draw?
2 Make a list of five careers that you think you could or would like to do based on the things you are good at.

Activity 3

In pairs, compare your careers lists from Activity 2. Each choose one career that interests you most and list five ways you could find out about this job.

Activity 4

Is it important to start thinking now about what you might want to do later in life? Give reasons for your answer.

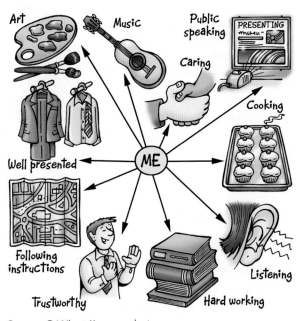

Source 3 What I'm good at

10.7 How do I improve my prospects?

In this lesson you will:
- think about the types of jobs and careers that are available to you
- consider what motivates people to work
- identify what factors will motivate you.

Most people work at some time in their lives. There are various reasons for working, but for the majority of people it's because they need to earn money so that they can survive in society. Some people get extra job satisfaction because they enjoy the work that they do. Employers are keen to have people working for them who are motivated.

Starter

Why do you think it is important to be motivated by what you do? Try to think of at least five reasons.

Source 1 What motivates me to work?

> Relationships – enjoying being with the people you work with; having self-respect.

> Self-fulfilment – personal satisfaction, for example feeling that you are doing something interesting and worthwhile.

> Material comforts – the things you can buy with your salary, for example holidays, clothing, a car, etc.

> Status – gaining personal recognition; being in charge.

> Security – a secure job where you are unlikely to be made redundant.

Activity 1

Look at Source 1. It's not always possible to get each of these five things from one job. If you had to put the factors in order, which one would be most important to you – and why?

Form your own personal priority order in the shape of the Diamond Five shown in Source 2. The top factor should be the most important to you; the bottom one should be the least important.

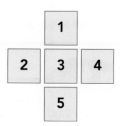

Source 2 Diamond Five

154

Activity 2

Now that you have thought about what motivates you to work, consider what that means for your chosen career.

Look at Source 3. Copy and complete the following table by placing each statement from Source 3 under the heading you think it fits best. Explain why you think it fits there.

Material comforts	Status	Relationships	Security	Self-fulfilment

Source 3 What do I want from my job?

a) To look after people	b) To work as part of a team	c) To be my own boss	d) To manage other people	e) Long summer holidays	f) Annual bonus payments
g) To decide how and when to do work	h) To stay in the same job for working life	i) To have good work colleagues	j) Not to have to take my work home with me	k) To be offered new opportunities	l) To receive recognition for my work
m) To get overtime payments	n) To be respected by fellow workers	o) To have good promotion prospects	p) To have good long-term prospects	q) To travel and stay in the best hotels	r) To do interesting work
s) To receive on-the-job training	t) To have a high level of responsibility	u) To get a new company car each year	v) To deal directly with customers	w) To receive good wages	x) To be able to see the results of my work

Activity 3

1   Look at the table headings from Activity 2. Choose the heading that represents the most important motivation you identified in your Diamond Five.
2   Now look at the statements that you placed underneath that heading and try to think of any jobs or careers that will give you the motivation and job satisfaction you are looking for.

S Specific (e.g. I will base my options choices on subjects I enjoy and can achieve in)
M Measurable (e.g. I will be on time each day this term)
A Attainable (e.g. I will finish projects by their deadline)
R Realistic (e.g. I will research which qualifications I need for my career path)
T Time specific (e.g. I will achieve these targets by the date I have to choose my options)

Source 4 SMART targets

Activity 4

Look at Source 4. Now write down a specific next step for yourself that fits one of the SMART target criteria and will help you on your way to your future career.

10.8 What does the law say about work?

In this lesson you will:
- think about some of the jobs teenagers can do
- learn about some of the rules affecting teenagers and work
- consider some of the pressures that can arise when working and studying at the same time.

Source 1 Typical teenage jobs

Starter

Look at Source 1. What are some of the typical jobs a teenager could do? Name one important skill and one important quality needed for each job.

Source 2 Teenagers working part time in England: the rules

School days	Not more than 2 hours in one day during the following periods: Morning: 7am to start of school or Evening: close of school to 7pm
Saturdays	Up to 5 hours between 7am and 7pm
Sundays	Up to 2 hours between 7am and 11am
Term time (including weekends)	Up to a maximum of 12 hours a week (including weekends)
School holidays (including weekends)	Up to a maximum of 25 hours a week 5 hours a day, 7am–7pm on any day except Sunday On Sundays, 2 hours, 7am–7pm

NB The rules in Source 2 apply to thirteen to fourteen-year-olds. Fifteen to sixteen-year-olds may work for up to 8 hours on Saturdays and up to a maximum of 35 hours a week during school holidays.

Activity 1

Look at Source 2 and discuss the following questions:
1 Why were these laws made?
2 If you were to make any changes to them, what changes would you make and why?
3 Do you think a teenager working for their own family's business should have to follow these laws?

Many pupils want to work to help the family finances, but it is important that they do not do so much paid work that it harms their progress in school. In England there are strict rules about the hours that can be worked. There are exceptions for child actors, models and performers. Children working in these areas will need a performance licence. Everyone else has to adhere to the rules in Source 2.

Source 3 Two case studies

Lin has always done well at school and her parents have very high expectations of her. They really want her to be the first person in their family to go to university. Lin studies hard but her grades are low in some subjects. Her parents decide to send her for extra tuition. Lin isn't enjoying this: the tutor makes her feel stupid, she isn't sleeping well because of how worried she is and she has started feeling really bad about herself.

Activity 2

Look at Source 3 and answer the following questions:
1 What advice would you offer to Lin to help her feel less pressured?
2 If Patrick asked you how he should prioritise his choices, what would you say?
3 Do you agree that teenagers are under increasing pressure to achieve more in their studies and exam grades? Give reasons for your answers.

Patrick has a busy life. He socialises with his friends, works hard at school and has a part-time job to save up for the future. He is, however, getting exhausted. Patrick's boss wants him to work more shifts when there are big sales and more customers in the shop. Patrick would love the extra money but his mock exams are coming up soon.

Source 4 Children and employment

Children are not allowed to work:

- ✗ without an employment permit issued by the education department of the local council, if this is required by local bylaws
- ✗ in places like a factory or industrial site
- ✗ during school hours
- ✗ for more than one hour before school (unless local bylaws allow it)
- ✗ for more than 4 hours without taking a break of at least 1 hour
- ✗ in most jobs in pubs and betting shops and those prohibited in local bylaws
- ✗ in any work that may be harmful to their health, wellbeing or education
- ✗ without having a two-week break from any work during the school holidays in each calendar year.

Activity 3

Look at Source 4. Young people were not consulted when these rules and regulations were brought in.

1 Do these rules and regulations do enough to protect a young person's health and safety in the workplace?
2 If you could remove something from the list, what would it be and why?
3 If you could make a new rule for the list, what would it be and why?

Activity 4

Think back over the lesson and identify one important new fact about youth employment that you've learnt.

11.1 How do I save and how do I budget?

In this lesson you will learn:
- that managing your money can help you save
- how to set up a budget and cope with the unexpected.

Starter

Some people say about money, 'Easy come, easy go'. Is that really true? As a Year 7 pupil you are not yet old enough to have a paid job, so where does your money come from? And when you've got it, what do you use it for?

Source 1

A spend, spend, spend person

A save, save, save person

A spend some, save some person

Activity 1

People have very different attitudes to what they do with their money.
In Source 1 are three types of people. In pairs, brainstorm the advantages and disadvantages of being each kind of person.

Activity 2

Imagine that you take a balanced approach to money and want to save some of it. Where do you think the best place is to save your money, and why?
- In a piggy bank
- In an ordinary account (often called a 'current account')
- In a savings account
- In a stocks and shares portfolio

After one year, if you don't take any money out, what do you think will have happened to your money?

Source 2

✓	Birthday present for Mum or Dad
✓	Pizza out with friends
✓	Donation to a charity collection box
✓	Entertainment activity with friends (cinema?)
✓	Latest fashion item of clothing – just like friends have
✓	Lend money to a friend who needs it
✓	New music download
✓	Sweets/Ice cream/Crisps
✓	Top-up mobile phone

Activity 3

In Activity 2 you were thinking about a balanced approach involving savings. How can we balance our approach when it comes to spending? One way is to think about our priorities. In Source 2 are nine things that you might spend your money on. In pairs, rank them in order of priority. Remember that you will have a limited amount to spend, so you will have to make some choices.

Activity 4

Sam is trying to work out how he can afford to go away on a camping trip. At present he spends all his income each week. He needs to save a total of £20 in the next ten weeks.

1 How much does he need to save per week?
2 What are the different ways of saving this amount per week?
3 Copy and complete Table 1, filling in the figures for him.
4 Discuss your solutions with the class.

Table 1

Current weekly income	£	Current weekly spending	£
pocket money	2	comic	1
money for odd jobs	2	pet food	1
		music	2
TOTAL	4	TOTAL	4
New weekly income		**New weekly spending**	
		Weekly savings target	
TOTAL		TOTAL	

Activity 5

Look at Table 2, which shows how Sam and three friends budget to go on a trip.

Suddenly one friend drops out. Table 3 shows how this affects their finances. The petrol money and the campsite fee are 'fixed costs' that can't be reduced, even if there are fewer people.

1 Work out the rest of the budget.
2 What effect does one person dropping out have on their budget?
3 What changes to the budget can you suggest to make it balance?

Table 2 Sam's and his friends' budget for equally sharing the trip costs

Original budget			
Income	£	Spending	£
Sam	20	Petrol money for lift to and from campsite	16
Friend 1	20	Campsite fee	10
Friend 2	20	Food, etc. at £10 each	40
Friend 3	20	Entry money – local attraction at £2.50 each	10
		Ice creams at £1 each	4
TOTAL	80	TOTAL	80

Table 3 Revised budget

Income	£	Spending	£
Sam	20	Petrol money for lift to and from campsite	16
Friend 1	20	Campsite fee	10
Friend 2	20	Food, etc. at £10 each	
		Entry money – local attraction at £2.50 each	
		Ice creams at £1 each	
TOTAL	60	TOTAL	

Activity 6

As you saw in Activity 5, sudden changes may affect your budget. How would you make sure your budget was robust enough to withstand a 'rainy day'?

11.2 What influences our spending?

In this lesson you will learn:
- some of the reasons why we spend money
- how we choose to support different kinds of shops
- how price and competition affect our consumer decisions
- how our consumer decisions affect other people.

Starter

Why do we spend money? In pairs, list all the things you've bought over the last week. Then discuss how much you needed the things, and whether they were luxury or impulse purchases.

Activity 1

1 As a class, brainstorm all the different types of shops you can think of.
2 Now think about how you decide where to shop. Imagine you are a typical customer at each of the shops shown in Source 1. In pairs, list all the reasons why you'd choose to shop at each, then give feedback to the class.

The Starter activity should have got you thinking about what people of your age spend their money on and why. You are consumers and have choices about what you buy and where you buy things. You make decisions that have an impact on the economy.

Small independent local grocery shop

Large out-of-town supermarket

Designer boutique

Local speciality shop

Charity shop

Source 1 Different shops

Your decision on where to spend your money doesn't just affect that particular shop. It also affects all the suppliers who provide goods and services to that shop, and it affects the other shops that you choose not to use. The different effects are shown in Source 2.

Activity 2

Look at Source 2 and answer the following questions:

1 What would happen if consumers could get all they needed at the supermarket, and stopped using the small independent grocery shop and local speciality shops?

2 If everyone started to buy at the charity shop and no one went to the designer boutique, what might be the effects?

Source 2

Shops	Small independent grocery shop	Large out-of-town supermarket	Designer boutique	Local speciality shop	Charity shop
Suppliers	Medium and mass market suppliers	Mass market suppliers from across UK and abroad	Design industry (clothing and goods)	Individual or small-scale suppliers from locality	People donating goods
		Advertising industry	Advertising industry	Local advertising	
		Packaging industry	Packaging industry		
		Finance industry	Finance industry		

Activity 3

1 In Activity 1, you looked at what factors affect our decisions as to where to shop. As a class, discuss whether price is the most important of those factors.

2 If price is important, imagine what would happen if one supermarket chain slashed its prices for milk. In pairs, work out a possible chain reaction in answer to these questions:
   a Would people buy more milk there?
   b What would happen to milk sales at other supermarkets and at the small grocery shop?
   c Would these other shops put their prices down, too? If not, how could they compete?
   d What impact would this have on the dairy farmers who supply the supermarket?
   e Would the consumer pay more for local milk?
   f What might make milk prices go back up again?

3 When shops compete with each other over price, there are winners and losers. As a class, name all the possible winners and losers, giving an explanation for each one.

Activity 4

On your own, list three things that you have learnt that a shop can do to persuade you to buy its goods rather than those from another shop.

11.3 How enterprising am I?

Some of you may have watched the TV programme *Dragons' Den*. You may not know that it was first launched on television in Japan. *Dragons' Den* is now an international brand with versions airing in countries across the globe. In the programme, members of the public with ideas for new business ventures pitch for investment in the Den from the Dragons. These members of the public are enterprising people, that is they have used their creativity to develop new business ideas. The Dragons are business people who are willing to invest their own money in exchange for a share of the new business.

Source 1 Two enterprising and successful people who pitched in the *Dragons' Den*

Name: Richard Blakesley and Chris Barnardo
Pitching: The Wand Company
Investment required: £200,000
Investment secured: £200,000 for 30% of the company
Brief description: A universal remote control that looks like a magic wand. (The Wand Company has also released products including a Doctor Who Sonic Screwdriver.)

Name: Levi Roots
Pitching: Reggae Reggae Sauce
Investment required: £50,000 for 20% of the company
Investment secured: £50,000 for 40% of the company
Brief description: Hot spicy barbecue sauce and seasonings

Starter

Look at Source 1. It shows enterprising and successful people who pitched in *Dragons' Den* with two very different products.
Have you ever wanted to invent anything?
Work with a partner to share your ideas.

Finding innovative and successful new products and services isn't easy. A good way to get started is to decide on your target group and then identify the services and products they might wish to buy.

Activity 1

This exercise will help you formulate ideas for a new business. Look at Source 2 which shows working mothers as a target group.

1 Copy the hexagon outline on to a large sheet of paper.
2 Choose a new target group (for example teenage boys, toddlers, retired people) and write it in the centre of your diagram.
3 You will need to think about the lifestyle of this new group and add these aspects to your diagram.
4 For each lifestyle aspect, show the products and services that the people in your target market would find useful. How could these be developed into a new business idea?

Source 2 Business ideas

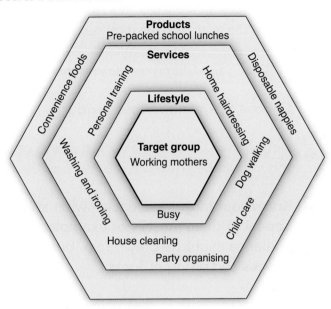

Source 3 A business plan

BUSINESS PLAN
Business name:
What will your business be called?
Business idea:
What is the product or service?   What is its potential to be successful?   What competition will there be from others?   How do you limit the risks involved?   How will the product/service be promoted?   What will you charge?
Target market:
Whom is the product/service aimed at?   Why are these customers likely to buy it?
Finance:
What will you need money for?   Where might you get this money?

Activity 2

Now that you have an idea for a business you need to write a business plan. An example of how you can write one is given in Source 3.

This will show potential investors that the business is worth investing in. In *Dragons' Den* it is the product and the business plan together that form the pitch.

Activity 3

Now that you have your product/service and business plan ready, you need to devise a pitch for funds to start running your business.

Prepare a pitch that lasts no more than two minutes. You can use a variety of media to do this.

Finally, present your pitch to the rest of the class.

Dragons' Den was used as a model to explore some ideas about business planning. Now you will use some ideas from *The Apprentice* – a series that sets its candidates a series of challenging tasks. One of the challenges in each series is to devise an effective advertising campaign to launch a new product or service. Groups work in teams and nominate a project manager who is responsible for leading the task. At the end of the task, the candidates are called to the boardroom. The team with the most successful campaign wins.

Lord Alan Sugar

Source 4 Planning an advert to promote your product

1 Choose the name of your product.

2 Define the USP (unique selling point) of your product – this should be the main message of the advert.

3 Know your target audience – what style of advert will appeal to them most? For example, a younger audience might be drawn to a 'busy' advert with lots of images and different fonts.

4 Choose the images that you want to appear in your advert – will they be of the product or of something else?

5 Decide where the images and text should go.

Activity 4

Working in groups, choose one of the products or services from your *Dragons' Den* ideas that you thought were worth funding. Devise an advertising plan for promoting this product/service. Use Source 4 as a guide.

Remember to choose a good name for your product or business.

Activity 5

Now that you have your advertising plan, in your groups, design and prepare the advert itself. You will need to ensure that you follow the plan closely. Remember to put your USP (unique selling point) across to your audience effectively.

Check your finished advert to ensure it meets all the criteria you set out in your plan.

Activity 6

In this lesson you have been thinking about marketing. You have also had the opportunity to develop your group work skills.
Look at Source 5. Read the questions carefully on your own and give each section a score.

Source 5 A self-assessment chart

	Successful group work qualities	How did we do? Questions to ask ourselves	Self-assessment: score out of 5 5 = excellent 1 = poor
Working together	• Doing my best • Helping others to do their best • Not giving up	• How much did team members encourage each other? • Did the team give up?	
Motivation	• Using good communication skills • Being supportive of each other all the time • Using lots of different skills	• Did we listen to each other? • Did we discuss how to share the tasks? • Did we remain supportive throughout?	
Thinking	• Being creative • Trying new ideas	• Did we discuss various answers and solutions? • Did we offer any new ideas?	
Completing the task	• Seeing it through to the end • Keeping focused on the task • Everyone participating	• Did we complete the task on time? • Did we complete the task successfully? • Did everyone contribute?	

Activity 7

Consider the pitches that were made in your version of *Dragons' Den* and the marketing you did as part of *The Apprentice* task.
Take a vote as a whole class: which idea was most worth funding and why?

Index

A

abuse 44–5, 75, 104, 105
alcohol 47, 48, 50, 51–2, 55
assertiveness/aggressiveness 62–3, 117

B

bereavement 76–7
body image 68–9
budgeting 159–61
bullying 94–5, 139
business plans 165

C

careers/jobs 148–55
Childline 65, 108, 139
Children's Commissioner for England 108
child sexual exploitation (CSE) 103, 105
commitment 40–1
communication 37, 92–3, 115, 144–5
condoms 23, 27
confidentiality 23, 86–7
contraception 22–3
coping strategies 11, 42, 65, 90, 107

D

diet 79, 82–3
difference 124–5
discrimination 140–1

E

enterprise 164–7
equality 32–3, 130, 131
Every Child Matters (ECM) 118

F

families 74–5, 84, 112–15
feelings/emotions 30–1, 70–2, 111, 116–17

female genital mutilation (FGM) 104, 105
finances 157, 159–63
forced marriage 105
four Cs 42
FRANK (National Drugs Helpline) 53
friendship 34–5

G

gambling 98–9
gang culture 103, 105
goal-setting 146–7
golden rules 125, 129
Group Agreement 8–9

H

healthy living 78–9
helping hand 107
HIV/AIDS 24–5
homophobia 104, 105

I

identity 110–11, 122–5
illegal drugs 53, 54–5
immunisations 85

K

knife crime 102, 105

L

legal drugs 46–7: *see also* alcohol; tobacco
legal issues 20, 28–9, 41, 43, 47, 54–5, 120, 156–8
loss 76–7

M

media 38–9, 48–9, 79: *see also* social media
mediation 134
medicines 52–3, 54, 55
mental health 64–5
motivation 152, 154

P

personal health profile 80–1
personal qualities 60–1, 111
personal safety 45, 102–5
pornography 39
positive risk 58, 88, 96–7
prejudice 125, 140–1
problems 106–9, 132–4
puberty 18–19, 30–1

R

recovery position 100
refusal skills 42–3, 92–3
reproduction 20–1
resilience 66–7, 73
respect 33, 115
responsibilities 8–9, 120–1
rights 8–9, 86, 120–1, 130–1
risks 56–9, 88–91, 96–101

S

Samaritans 65, 138
sexually transmitted infections (STIs) 26–7
sleep 84
SMART targets 147, 155
social media 29, 34, 38, 101, 137
solvents 46, 47, 50, 55

T

tobacco 47, 50, 51, 55

U

United Nations Convention on the Rights of the Child 120–1
Universal Declaration of Human Rights 130–1

V

values 8–9, 14–17, 125
voluntary agencies 138–9
volunteering 135–7